The best of
MILAN

ROWLAND·MEAD

NEW
HOLLAND

GLOBETROTTER™

First edition published in 2006
by New Holland Publishers (UK) Ltd
London • Cape Town • Sydney • Auckland
10 9 8 7 6 5 4 3 2 1

website: www.newhollandpublishers.com

Garfield House, 86 Edgware Road
London W2 2EA
United Kingdom

80 McKenzie Street
Cape Town 8001
South Africa

14 Aquatic Drive
Frenchs Forest, NSW 2086
Australia

218 Lake Road
Northcote, Auckland
New Zealand

Distributed in the USA by
The Globe Pequot Press, Connecticut

ISBN 1 84537 218 2

Publishing Manager (UK): Simon Pooley
Publishing Manager (SA): Thea Grobbelaar
DTP Cartographic Manager: Genené Hart
Editor: Thea Grobbelaar
Cover design: Nicole Bannister
Cartographer: Tanja Spinola
Picture Researcher: Shavonne Johannes
Proofreader: Alicha van Reenen

Reproduction by Fairstep (Pty) Ltd, Cape Town
Printed and bound by Times Offset (M) Sdn. Bhd.,
Malaysia.

Photographic Credits:
**alamarphotography/photographersdirect.
com:** pages 16, 70, 76; **Antonio De Luca,
Milano/photographersdirect.com:** page 20;
FAN/jonarnold.com: cover; **Axiom/Renzo
Frontoni:** pages 17, 19, 84; **International
Photobank/Peter Baker:** title page, pages 8,
47, 50, 69, 83; **International Photobank/
Gary Goodwin:** page 49; **Caroline Jones:**
page 63; **Rowland Mead:** pages 7, 11, 15, 30,
41, 78, 82; **OJPHOTOS.COM/photographers
direct.com:** pages 6, 43, 46; **Alberto Ramella/
photographersdirect.com:** pages 21, 26, 27,
29, 33, 44, 45, 52, 54, 71, 72, 73, 81; **Richard
Sale:** pages 22, 25, 28, 31, 32, 34, 35, 36, 37,
39, 40; **Jeroen Snijders:** pages 9, 12, 13, 14,
23, 24, 51, 60, 64, 67, 80, 91; **Richard
Wareham/photographersdirect.com:** pages
18, 42, 53, 74, 75;

Front Cover: *Theatre-goers relax in one of
Milan's elegant cafés.*
Title Page: *The Duomo, Milan's cathedral.*

CONTENTS

MAKE THE MOST OF YOUR GUIDE

Reading these two pages will help you to get the most out of your guide and save you time when using it. Sites discussed in the text are cross-referenced with the cover maps – for example, the reference 'Map C–D4' refers to the Central Milan Map (Map C), column D, row 4. Use the Map Plan below to quickly locate the map you need.

MAP PLAN

Outside Back Cover

Outside Front Cover

Inside Front Cover

Inside Back Cover

THE BIGGER PICTURE

Key to Map Plan

A – Milan Metro Map
B – Around Milan
C – Central Milan
D – Milan and the
    Italian Lakes
E – Como
F – Pavia
G – Bergamo
H – Mantua

Key to Symbols

⊠ — address

☎ — telephone

Ⴙ — fax

🖳 — website

🖰 — e-mail address

🕘 — opening times

🚍 — transport

💰 — entry fee

🍴 — restaurants nearby

M — nearest metro station

Map Legend

motorway	══S415══	motorway	════════	
national road	Passo del Vivione	main road	**Via Ariosto**	
main road	══S369══	pedestrian mall	VIA D CHIOSTRI	
minor road	═══════	other road	Via Torino	
railway	───────	built-up area		
boundary	▬▬▬▬▬	hotel	(H) THE GRAY	
water	Dam / Rio Guediana	building of interest	Palazzo Reale	
city	**MILAN**	library		
major town	⊙ **Pavia**	shopping	(S) Galleria Vittorio Emanuele II	
small town	○ Como	metro station	Ⓜ Duomo	
large village	◎ Ghedi	post office	⊠	
village	○ Verenna	parking area	P	
airport	✈ ✈ M. Alban	tourist information	i	
peak	▲ 2019 m	one way arrow	↓	
cable car	•——•	place of worship	△ San Sisto	
place of interest	● Pinacoteca	police station	●	
viewpoint	⋟	bus terminus	🚌	
campsite	⚠	hospital	⊕	
golf course	⌐	park & garden	Parco Sempione	

Keep us Current

Travel information is apt to change, which is why we regularly update our guides. We'd be most grateful to receive feedback from you if you've noted something we should include in our updates. If you have any new information, please share it with us by writing to the Publishing Manager, Globetrotter, at the office nearest to you (addresses on the imprint page of this guide). The most significant contribution to each new edition will be rewarded with a free copy of the updated guide.

Above: *A roofscape view of Milan, with the Alps as the city's backdrop.*

MILAN

Many people consider that the wealthy city of Milan should really be the capital of Italy, since it is the industrial and commercial powerhouse of the country. It differs from the somnolent south of Italy – no long siestas for the Milanese, who like to see themselves as being more northern European in attitude. They pride themselves on their timekeeping, their industry and their ability to make things function properly. Milan's population of 1.4 million accounts for barely four per cent of the Italian people and yet they contribute around a quarter of the country's tax returns!

The Land
Mountains and Rivers

Located on the fertile **Lombardy Plain** drained by the River Po, Milan's backdrop is the snowcapped **Alps**. Today, the Po Valley is the richest agricultural region in Italy, growing rice, grapes, maize and a wide variety of fruit and vegetables. The **River Po**, which is Italy's longest river, has also been important for navigation, and large ships can still reach as far inland as Pavia, just 38km (24 miles) south of Milan.

To the south of the Po Valley are the **Apennine Hills**, which form the spine of Italy. On a clear day it is possible to stand on the Apennines and see the magnificent wall of the Alps rising above the haze of the Po Valley.

The River Po
With a length of 405km (251 miles), the River Po is Italy's longest river. It rises in the Cottian Alps and enters the Adriatic Sea south of Venice. It is navigable as far as Pavia. Its main tributaries are the Ticino, the Adda and the Adige. The River Po plain is the richest agricultural area in Italy. It is also Italy's most polluted river – 136,000 tonnes of nitrates, 250 tonnes of arsenic and 60 tonnes of mercury are pumped into the river daily.

Fauna and Flora

Don't expect to see much **wildlife** in **Milan**, apart from the thousands of pigeons that inhabit its squares and a few bedraggled specimens of wildfowl on the lakes in the city's parks. The situation is little better on the **Lombardy Plain**, where during the hunting season from August to March, and particularly on Sundays, the fields reverberate with the thunder of guns as hunters with their feathered Alpine hats blast at everything that moves, whether the creature is protected or not.

Around the **lakes**, the situation improves, with a variety of water birds and fish. At the northern end of the lakes, on the approach to the **Alps**, the amount of wildlife increases. The coniferous forests are the habitat of a variety of mammals.

However, it is the **flora** that draws many visitors to northern Italy, particularly in spring and early summer. The mild winter climate of the lakes (Garda has only frozen over once and that was in 1701) means that a wide range of exotic flowers, shrubs and trees can be grown in the gardens and hotel grounds along the waterside. The gardens on Isola Madre and Isola Bella on the Borromean Islands of Lake Maggiore are a wonderful example. Try not to miss the azaleas and rhododendrons at Villa Carlotta on Lake Como – they are truly spectacular during the early summer months of April and May.

Climate
The average January temperature in Milan is 1.9°C (35°F) and winters can be raw. Precipitation is light, but there is some snowfall in most years. Fog can linger for days on end. The average July temperature is 24.8°C (76°F) and it is even higher in August, when the humidity can be trying. Thunderstorms can be expected in late summer. May and September are the most pleasant months for sightseeing.

Below: *There is little in the way of wildlife in the city, but there are plenty of pigeons for tourists to feed.*

Below: *In the centre of the Piazza della Scala stands this monument to Leonardo da Vinci. Beneath his statue, on the corners of the plinth, are four of his best-known students: Botraffio, Salaino, Oggione and Da Sesto.*

History in Brief

Milan was probably founded around 600BC by the Insubres, who were a Celtic tribe from Gaul. In 222BC, the Romans arrived in the area, and Milan became the major settlement of Cisalpine Gaul, the Empire's second largest city after Rome. In AD313, Constantine issued the Edict of Milan, which officially recognized Christianity as a religion. Thereafter the city became an important religious centre, helped by the appointment of the well-respected Sant' Ambrogio (Ambrose) as Bishop of Milan.

The fall of the Roman Empire marked a period of decline for Milan. It was invaded by the Lombards, and again in 774 by the Franks led by Charlemagne. In 1045, Milan declared itself a *comune* or city-state.

The 13th century saw the first dynastic family come to power. This was the Torriani family, part of the pro-papal faction. They were defeated in 1277 by the Viscontis, the greatest of whom was Gian Galeazzo (1351–1402) who bought the title of Duke of Milan and also commissioned the building of the Duomo, Castello and many palaces. Gian Galeazzo died from the plague in 1402 and within 40 years the dynasty had died out.

Milan then came under the control of Francesco Sforza. The castle was rebuilt and renamed the Castello Sforzesco, and work was started on the Ospedale Maggiore. The golden age of the Sforzas came with Francesco's son Ludovico el Moro, who was a great patron of the arts. He brought to his court such talents as Leonardo da Vinci (1452–1519) and the architect Donato Bramante (1444–1514) who restored many of Milan's churches.

Ludovico was forced out of power in 1499 by Louis XII, who marched into Milan and claimed the city for himself. The population, weary of paying taxes to support the Sforza regime, welcomed Louis with open arms, while Ludovico spent the rest of his life in exile.

For the next three centuries Milan languished under foreign powers. The best to emerge from this period was San Carlo Borromeo (1538–84). A patron of the arts, he built numerous churches and social institutions for the poor, and got rid of corruption.

Above: *The massive statue of San Carlo Borromeo towers over the south end of Lake Maggiore to the northwest of Milan.*

Milan was ruled in turn by the French, the Spanish, the Austrians and again the French. Napoleon proclaimed the Cisalpine Republic and in 1800 crowned himself King of Italy in Milan Cathedral. He modernized the city, reformed the administration and set up schools on the *lycée* model. But the people were heavily taxed and many art treasures were removed to France, so the Milanese were not too unhappy when the Napoleonic Empire collapsed and Austrian forces returned in 1814. Austrian control was officially recognized at the Congress of Vienna in 1815, and the Habsburgs were to remain in charge of the city for the next 50 years.

Movements for uniting the country began to appear. The most influential figures were Giuseppe Mazzini (1805–72), an important political agitator; Giuseppe Garibaldi (1807–82), a charismatic military figure; and Count Camillo Cavour (*see* panel). In March 1848 the Milanese staged a revolt known as *Cinque Giornate* – the five days that the revolt lasted. The insurrection was crushed by the Austrians, but supported by Louis

Cavour (1810–61)
Count Camillo Benso di Cavour was the brains behind the unification of Italy. He was born in Turin, but for many years he worked for the Kings of Sardinia. It was to his great personal satisfaction that when Italy was united, Victor Emmanuel II of Sardinia became its first king. An able politician, Cavour believed that progress lay not in revolution, but in social and economic progress. Sadly, he died a year after Italy achieved unification.

OVERVIEW

Above: *The Italian flag has green, white and red vertical sections and is flown at all official functions.*

Napoleon, they were defeated at Magenta in 1859 and the north of Italy was united under Piedmont. **Victor Emmanuel II** of Piedmont marched into Milan through the triumphal arch that was built by Napoleon and which is now known as the Arch of Peace. He was proclaimed King of Italy in February 1861. Complete unity was achieved with the addition of Venice in 1866 and Rome in 1871. Milan was now the business and commercial capital of the newly united country.

World War I was a disaster for Italy. Its army was ill-equipped and of the 5.5 million Italians who were mobilized an estimated 40 per cent were killed or wounded.

Mussolini took Italy into **World War II**, making a pact with Hitler. In 1943 Milan became a target for Allied bombers, which inflicted heavy damage on the city. Meanwhile the Italians had formed a Resistance movement to harass the Germans. These partisans finally caught Mussolini as he was trying to escape to Switzerland (*see* panel).

In 1946 Victor Emmanuel III abdicated and Italy voted in a referendum to abolish the monarchy. The postwar period was typified by political instability – there were nearly 60 governments between 1946 and 1999. Milan, however, led the postwar 'economic miracle'.

The early 1990s brought bribery and corruption scandals and Milan became known as *Tangentopoli* or 'Bribe City'. Milan also produced Silvio Berlusconi, a media mogul and, in 2001, the country's prime minister.

Benito Mussolini and Fascism

It was not surprising that after World War I there was considerable social and economic unrest in Italy and the Fascist movement came to the fore. Both the Fascist movement and its leader, Benito Mussolini, had close links with Milan. Mussolini became dictator of Italy in 1922 and his plans for buying weapons of war made him popular with the middle-class industrialists of Milan. As Mussolini was trying to escape to Switzerland at the end of World War II, he was shot along with his mistress, and his body was later strung up from the roof of a petrol station in Milan's Piazza Loreto, the place where some partisans had been shot a few weeks earlier.

10

Government and Economy

Government

Since 1946 Italy has been a democratic republic. Government resides in Rome where the president is largely a figurehead. The decision-making is carried out by the lower house, known as the Chamber of Deputies. The upper house consists of senators from the 21 different regions of Italy. The regions also have a measure of self-government. Each region is divided into provinces. The lowest level of government is the local council or *comune*.

The Economy

A grasp of the contrasts between the north and south of Italy is essential in understanding the Italian economy. The south of the peninsula is on the fringe of Europe, with all the disadvantages of industrial location and transportation. It is hot and dry and lacking in energy, raw materials and resources. In addition it is dominated by the Mafia, whose influence extends into all parts of daily life, preventing initiative, enterprise and investment. In complete contrast, the north, based on the industrial triangle of Milan, Turin and the port of Genoa, is the powerhouse of modern Italy. The climate is more favourable for agriculture, and there are power sources in the form of natural gas and hydroelectricity.

Milan, itself with a population of around two million, is the country's economic capital. With its thriving industry, fashion

Political Parties
Italy has many political parties. The largest are the right-of-centre **Christian Democratic Union (UDC)**, the left-wing **Partito Socialista Italiano (PSI)** and the right-wing **National Alliance**, noted for anti-immigration policies. Some parties are regionally based, such as the **Liga Nord** with its stronghold in the Plain of Lombardy. There are also several small parties, including the **Radical Party**, whose candidate, the porn star La Cicciolina, recently won a seat.

Below: *The Pirelli Building is a symbol of the city's postwar reconstruction.*

Voting
Every Italian is expected to vote as his/her civic duty, although there is no penalty for failing to do so. In fact, Italy has a higher turnout at elections than any other European country – often over 90 per cent. The proportional representation system and the large number of political parties in existence led to a vast number of coalition governments in the postwar period. In 1993 a new system was introduced whereby 75 per cent of the upper and lower houses were elected by the first-past-the-post system, with the remaining 25 per cent elected by proportional representation. This has led to more political stability. Sylvio Berlusconi's recent government, for example, lasted for 1410 days – a record for postwar Italy.

houses, stock exchange and artistic heritage, it is a major European city. The Milanese and their fellow northerners feel that they are subsidizing the south, and there is talk of federalism or partition, but after a hard-won unification campaign, this is unlikely.

The People
Language
Much of the Italian language is derived from Latin, so that visitors with a knowledge of French or Spanish will find the basics easy to pick up, particularly as each syllable is pronounced as it is seen and no letter is silent. There are vast numbers of regional dialects in Italy, and it was not until Dante wrote in the Tuscan dialect that this became the educated form of Italian to use. Some Italians even speak a different language – German is used in the Alto Adige region and French is spoken in the Valle d'Aosta. The media, however, and particularly television, are gradually eradicating Italy's linguistic diversity.

Few Italians are very good linguists, but the ability to speak good English confers some status. Visitors should find that in the tourist industry there is sure to be someone in most of the hotels and restaurants who speaks an adequate level of English. Nevertheless, the ability of visitors to speak a few words of Italian will be greeted with smiles of pleasure.

THE PEOPLE

Religion

The Roman Catholic church has been a dominant factor in Italian life for centuries and it still subtly permeates society today, although it no longer has the political power or social influence that it had in the past. Today, although 97 per cent of Italians are baptized and church marriages are the norm, fewer than 10 per cent regularly attend Mass. The strict rules of the past have been relaxed – both contraception and abortion are readily available, and the barriers to divorce have largely been removed. Despite this trend, the support for saints' days is undiminished, perhaps because all Italians enjoy a good party. Most saints' days involve a religious procession, when a statue of the saint is paraded through the streets. These are particularly atmospheric at Easter.

The Family

The family has always been a major influence in Italian life, probably due to the country's agricultural past and the need for cooperation in order to survive, plus the teachings of the Catholic church. Today, children, particularly males, tend to live at home until their thirties. Most students attend their local university and continue to reside at home, maintaining the traditional link between mother and son. In Italy the matriarchal structure is alive and well!

The north of Italy has seen a weakening of the family structure in recent decades, due to social changes such as a lower birth rate, the availability of divorce, and geographical migration in search of work. In the south, however, the family is as strong as ever.

Above: *Milan's fashion shows are renowned the world over.*
Opposite: *Senior citizens are respected and well provided for in northern Italy.*

Giuseppe Verdi
Born in Parma, Verdi moved to Milan at an early age and spent most of his life here. He failed to gain entrance to the conservatoire, which ironically now bears his name. He is known almost entirely for his operas, most of which had their debuts at La Scala, including *Rigoletto* (1851), *La Traviata* (1853), *Aïda* (1871) and *Otello* (1887). Verdi made his home in the Grand Hotel et de Milan, where he died in what is now suite 107.

☆ See Map C–E4	★ ★ ★

The Duomo
✉ Piazza del Duomo
☎ 02 8646 3456
🕐 cathedral
07:00–19:00 daily,
roof 09:00–17:45
💰 cathedral free, roof
€5 by elevator, €3.50
by stairs
Ⓜ 1, 3, Duomo
🍽 restaurants nearby

THE DUOMO

Dominating the Piazza del Duomo is Milan's cathedral. As you emerge from the metro, you have a breathtaking view of the west front, with its pink-fringed marble and forest of pinnacles and statues. The sheer size of the cathedral is also impressive. It is claimed that the Duomo is the third largest cathedral in the world after Seville in Spain and St Peter's in Rome. It is also the only Gothic cathedral of any note in Italy.

The most photographed part of the Duomo is the ornate west front or **façade**. Six huge vertical buttresses divide this triangular shape into five sections, each of which is capped with a range of pinnacles.

The **interior** has five aisles supported by 52 pillars (said to represent the weeks of the year). The capitals on each pillar are, unusually, decorated with statues of the saints. The exceptional stained glass varies in age from 15th century to modern. On the floor at the west end is a **meridian** placed there by the Brera astronomers in 1786. Along the south aisle you can appreciate the stunning stained glass. In the north transept is a gruesome **statue of St Bartholomew**. Dating from 1562, it shows the saint, having been flayed alive, carrying his own skin!

History of the Duomo
The Duomo was begun in 1386 by Gian Galeazzo Visconti, but took another 500 years to complete. The main spire, with its golden Madonna, was added in the 18th century, and Napoleon completed the west façade in 1813. Even in the 20th century, work was being carried out on the roof and the five bronze doors on the façade.

See Map C–E4 ★★★

Walk towards the altar and take the door leading to the **crypt**. For a small fee you can see the room where an octagonal Baroque vault contains the remains of San Carlo Borromeo, the 16th-century Bishop of Milan. Back on ground level, walk along the choir aisle, noting the funerary **monument to Gian Giacomo Medici**. In the vault above the choir a small red light marks the niche where a nail from Christ's cross is kept.

Entering the ambulatory, don't miss the **southern sacristy door**, which dates from 1393 and has superb carvings and inscriptions. The **apse** is generally considered to be the most beautiful part of the cathedral. Its three magnificent windows have delicate tracery and fine 19th-century glass. The ambulatory leads to the north transept, dominated by the monumental early 13th-century **Trivulzio Candelabrum**, attributed to French goldsmith Nicholas de Verdun. The vast 4.87m (16ft) candelabrum has seven branches and sits on a decorated stone base.

Along the north aisle, you pass the **Chapel of the Crucifix**, which contains the nail that San Carlo Borromeo carried in a procession to thwart the plague of 1576 (*see* panel). Take the steps down to the octagonal **baptistry** where Sant'Ambrogio is reputed to have baptized St Augustine in AD387.

Don't miss the **roof terraces**. The stairs can be avoided by using the lift (small fee) on the north side of the cathedral. The roof allows you to study the statues, spires and buttresses in detail. There are fine views over the city's rooftops and on a clear day you can even see the Alps in the distance.

Above: *In the Piazza del Duomo this imposing equestrian statue of Victor Emmanuel II faces the cathedral.*
Opposite: *The magnificent façade of Milan's Duomo.*

The Nail of the Holy Cross

Stand in the choir of the Duomo and look up into the vaulting. A small red light marks a niche that contains a nail reputed to come from Christ's cross. The nail is in the shape of a horseshoe and was found by St Helena. It eventually came into the possession of Sant' Ambrogio. San Carlo Borromeo carried the nail in the procession during the plague of 1576. Each September 14, the Bishop of Milan is carried heavenwards on a small platform with invisible pulleys (it must seem like a miracle!) to collect the nail and show it to the people of Milan.

HIGHLIGHTS

See Map C–E3   ★★★

Above: *La Scala, the world's most famous opera house.*

LA SCALA

Take a short walk through the Galleria from the Duomo and you will reach Piazza della Scala and the world's most famous opera house. The Teatro alla Scala derives its name from the Church of Santa Maria alla Scala that once stood on the site. The opera house was financed by Austrian Empress Maria Theresa and opened in 1778. All the world's most eminent conductors and opera singers have performed at La Scala and first nights here are a must for the great and good of Milan. The opera house was badly damaged during World War II, but it was quickly rebuilt. It reopened in 1946 under the conductorship of Arturo Toscanini.

In recent years La Scala has been closed for restoration, during which there was considerable controversy, particularly regarding the demolition of the backstage area. It reopened again in early 2005, but not without drama, as its new director swiftly resigned.

The **Museo la Scala** is normally located to the left of the main doors of the opera house (during renovation it was in temporary quarters in the Palazzo Busca in Corso Magenta). It has a fascinating collection of opera memorabilia, including items such as musical scores, costumes, model sets and paintings of several famous performers.

La Scala Opera House
✉ Piazza della Scala
☎ 02 7200 8027
🖥 www.teatrodella
scala.org
M 1, 3, Duomo
🍴 restaurants nearby

Museo La Scala
✉ Piazza della Scala
☎ 02 7200 8027
🕐 09:00–12:00 and
14:00–18:00 Tue–Sun

Santa Maria delle Grazie
✉ Piazza Santa Maria delle Grazie
☎ 02 4801 4248; to book for the *Last Supper* 02 8942 1146
🖥 www.cenacolo
viciano.it
🕐 08:00–14:00 Tue–Sat, 09:00–19:30 Sun
💰 the church is free, charge to see the *Last Supper* (no credit cards)
M 1, 2, Cadorna;
1, Conciliazione

See Map C–B3/B4   ★ ★ ★

SANTA MARIA DELLE GRAZIE

The exterior of the Church of Santa Maria delle Grazie is largely brick and is distinguished by the hemispherical dome on a cubic base. The church was built between 1463 and 1490 by Guiniforte Solari in a style described as a 'Gothic Renaissance transitional'. Ludovico el Moro later commissioned Bramante to make alterations, and the architect replaced the original apse with one in Renaissance style. The Great and Little Cloisters are charming. The latter leads to the sacristy, which is often used today for art exhibitions.

The refectory, which houses da Vinci's **Last Supper**, is entered by a separate door. (Opening times are notoriously variable and it is highly unlikely that you will gain immediate entry. You may even have to wait for the next day. It is advisable, therefore, to book ahead by telephone.) Painted by Leonardo for Ludovico el Moro between 1495 and 1497, it covers the entire rear wall of the refectory, measuring 9m (30ft) by 4.5m (14ft). It depicts the moment just after Christ said: 'One of you will betray me'. The painting began to deteriorate almost immediately and it has had some controversial restoration over the centuries. Note too the painting on the opposite wall of the refectory. It is Donato da Montafano's *Crucifixion*, which dates from 1495 and was commissioned by the Dominicans.

Painting the *Last Supper*

Fresco is a technique where the paint is applied to 'fresh' (fresco) mortar, which in drying binds the coloured pigment so that the painting becomes part of the wall itself. When Leonardo painted the *Last Supper* he tried a different technique, using tempera over a double layer of plaster. This proved faulty as the fresco could not withstand the dampness of the wall it was painted on, and very soon it began to decay. Experts tried heating the wall from behind, but this was unsuccessful. The fresco has been 'restored' so many times over the centuries that it is highly probable that little of Leonardo's original paintwork survives.

Below: *Leonardo da Vinci's* Last Supper, *on the refectory wall of the Church of Santa Maria delle Grazie.*

Castello Sforzesco
✉ Piazza Castello
☎ 02 8846 3700
🖥 www.milanocastello.it
🕐 08:00–20:00 daily (castle), 09:30–17:30 Tue–Sun (museums)
🔓 admission free
M 1, Cairoli-Cadorna; 2, Lanza-Cadorna

🌼 *See Map C–D3* | ★ ★ ★

CASTELLO SFORZESCO

This complex of brick buildings and towers, which in the past formed a formidable defensive fortress, now contains a series of excellent museums.

The castle has a long and fascinating history. It was built in 1368 by the Viscontis purely as a fortress, but it later became the ducal palace. During the short-lived Ambrosian Republic it was partially demolished, but rebuilt almost immediately by the Sforzas. Under Ludovico el Moro it evolved into a glittering Renaissance palace, in which Leonardo da Vinci and Bramante the architect worked. During the times of Spanish and Austrian occupation it reverted to the role of fortress. It was badly damaged during the Napoleonic era, but restored to its original 15th-century magnificence by Luca Beltrami in the 1890s. The castle was further damaged by bombs during World War II, necessitating more restoration in the postwar years.

Opposite: *Statues and other works of art abound at the Castello Sforzesco.*
Below: *The Milanese enjoy picnics in the shady grounds of Castello Sforzesco.*

The castle takes the shape of a square, with its massive walls pockmarked with holes at regular intervals. Once used for scaffolding, the holes now provide good homes for some of Milan's ubiquitous pigeons. The building's main façade facing the Largo Cairoli has a round tower at each corner. These towers

CASTELLO SFORZESCO

🌟 *See* Map C–D3   ★ ★ ★

reach 31m (100ft) high and bear the emblem of a snake, the symbol of the Sforza and Visconti families. Once water cisterns, the towers were given a military makeover in Beltrami's reconstructions. In the centre of the façade is the **Filarete Tower**, named after its designer. In 1521, this tower collapsed when the gunpowder that was stored there exploded. Beltrami rebuilt it from Filarete's original plans.

Pass the ornate computerized fountain and enter the main gateway under the Filarete Tower. This leads into the enormous Piazza D'Armi, the Sforza military training ground. Cross this courtyard and pass through a gateway. To the right is the Ducal Court containing the **Sforza Castle art galleries**. The first of these is the **Civic Museum of Art**, which is mainly given over to sculpture and tapestries. The prize exhibit has to be Michelangelo's *Rondanini Pietà*. The unfinished sculpture shows Mary struggling to hold up the body of the crucified Christ. On the other side of the courtyard in the upper storey is the **Pinacoteca**, which has a comprehensive collection of art from the 15th–18th centuries, including work by Bellini, Titian, Canaletto and a number of Lombard artists.

On the opposite side of the castle is the arcaded **Roccetta Courtyard**, which was always the last refuge in the event of a siege. The museum here has a collection of ancient Egyptian artefacts and local archaeological items.

Saved from Demolition
By the late 1800s the Castello Sforzesco was in a sad state of disrepair. The star-shaped bulwarks were knocked down during the French occupation and there was much talk of demolishing the whole of the remaining edifice. Its saviour was the Milanese architect **Luca Beltrami**. Between 1893 and 1904 he oversaw the castle's restoration, adding features that were not originally there, but accurately restoring other items, such as the tower which had collapsed in 1521. Beltrami's idea was that all of Milan's art collections should be housed at the Castello. Further restoration was needed after the considerable damage inflicted during World War II.

| ✿ See Map C–E4 | ★★★ |

Above: *The Galleria Vittorio Emanuele II, built in the late 19th century, is a stylish shopping arcade.*

GALLERIA VITTORIO EMANUELE II

This stylish shopping arcade has four arms, the south and north arms connecting the Piazza del Duomo with the Piazza della Scala. It was built between 1865 and 1877 to a design of Giuseppe Mengoni, who fell to his death from scaffolding shortly before it was opened.

The Galleria is entered through a squat 'triumphal arch', which leads to the central dome, made of iron and glass, and considered to be an engineering triumph in its day. Such was its success that similar *gallerie* were built in other Italian cities such as Rome and Naples. The Galleria is claimed to be the most exclusive shopping arcade in the country and is filled with fashion outlets, bookshops and restaurants. The elite of Milan like to be seen eating here after attending a performance at La Scala. Beneath the dome is Il Savini, considered to be the most exclusive restaurant in Milan. Amazingly, the diners at Il Savini have to look across to an American fast-food chain – an unfortunate juxtaposition.

Where the four arms of the Galleria meet there is an impressive mosaic sporting the coat of arms of Victor Emanuele's House of Savoy, and a large bull meant to symbolize Milan. It is a local tradition that passers-by step on the bull's testicles to guarantee good luck.

Galleria Vittorio Emanuele II
✉ Piazza del Duomo to Piazza della Scala
🕐 open 24 hours
M 1, 3, Duomo
🍴 various restaurants in the arcade

See Map C–C4 ★★★

SANT'AMBROGIO

Milan's best-known church can be found at the end of Via San Vittore next to a 12th-century gate, the **Pusterla di Sant'Ambrogio**. The building is dedicated to St Ambrose, the city's patron saint, who founded the church in 379. It has been enlarged and rebuilt many times, but what we see today dates mainly from the 1080s.

Sant'Ambrogio is considered to be the finest example of Romansque architecture in northern Italy and its pure architecture has been retained, with round arches found throughout the complex of buildings. The interior is severe, with red-brick vaulting setting off the white walls. An exception to this austerity is the golden altarpiece or *paliotto*, a 9th-century masterpiece by Volvinio, composed of four silver and gold panels encrusted with pearls and precious stones. Notice, too, the 11th-century pulpit above a Romano Christian sarcophagus. The remains of St Ambrose are in the crypt, along with those of Sts Gervasio and Protasio. The upper section of the portico (designed by Bramante) contains the **Museo della Basilica di Sant'Ambrogio**, which displays vestments, manuscripts, frescoes and even what is claimed to be the saint's bed.

Next door is the **Catholic University of the Sacred Heart** located in the former Bene-dictine monastery. The university was founded in 1921 and the building retains two of Bramante's cloisters.

Sant'Ambrogio
⊠ Piazza Sant' Ambrogio 15
☎ 02 8645 0895
🕐 Mon–Sat 07:30–12:00, 14:30–19:00; Sun 07:00–13:00, 15:00–20:00
🎟 admission free
M 2, Sant'Ambrogio

Museo della Basilica di Sant'Ambrogio
🕐 10:00–12:00 Mon, Wed–Fri, 15:00–17:00 Sat–Sun, closed Tue

Below: *Part of the lavish Lombard-Romanesque interior of Sant'Ambrogio, showing the gilded and bejewelled altarpiece.*

Pinacoteca di Brera
⊠ Via Brera 28
☎ 02 722 631
⊕ 08:30–19:15
Tue–Sun
♨ admission is charged, but entry is free for EU citizens under 18 or over 65
Ⓜ Lanza, Montenapoleone

Planetarium
⊠ Corso Venezia 57
☎ 02 8846 3341
⊕ open at times of shows – Tue and Thu 21:00, Sat and Sun 15:00 and 16:30

Museum of Natural History
⊠ Corso Venezia 55
☎ 02 8846 3280
⊕ 09:00–17:30 Tue–Fri, 09:00–18:00 Sat–Sun
Ⓜ Palestro

See Map C–E2   ★ ★ ★

PINACOTECA DI BRERA

The Brera area is one of the liveliest, most atmospheric parts of Milan. The winding, cobbled streets are full of art galleries, cafés and antique shops, while students from the Academy of Fine Art add to the colourful ambience. A good time to visit the quarter is on the third Saturday of each month when a flea market is held in the Via Brera.

The focus for most visitors to the Brera area will be the **Pinacoteca di Brera**, one of Italy's top art galleries. It is located in a palace that dates from 1773, although it is on the site of a much earlier monastery. Entry is via a rectangular courtyard with a double arcade of slender paired columns. In the centre of the cobbled courtyard is a bronze statue of Napoleon, who was largely responsible for bringing together the original collection from suppressed churches. The collection has since been augmented by donations. The paintings are mainly Italian and 90 per cent of those displayed are of a religious nature. Particularly important are Bramante's eight frescoes, Tintoretto's *Rediscovery of St Mark's Body*, the *Pietà* by Bellini, several Raphaels including *The Marriage of the Virgin*, and *Virgin With Child* by Piero della Francesca. Don't miss the foreshortened *Dead Christ* by Mantegna. The art gallery is on the first floor and is reached by steps leading from the courtyard.

Below: *Mantegna's unusual foreshortened painting of the* Dead Christ, *one of the star exhibits at the Pinacoteca di Brera.*

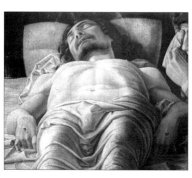

See Map C–F3 ★★

THE FASHION DISTRICT

Via Monte Napoleone, Via Manzoni, Via Sant' Andrea and Via della Spiga enclose the Quadrilatero d'Oro, Milan's famous fashion district. Here the shops of some of the top international fashion designers are interspersed with aristocratic palaces, tearooms and antique shops. Names such as Armani, Gucci, Versace, Chanel and Cardin ensure that this district is a Mecca for serious shoppers and spenders.

Above: *A window display in the Quadrilatero d'Oro.*

If you want more than window shopping you could take advantage of a new service. It had been noticed that many businessmen brought their wives to Milan, so agencies have been set up to provide guides to take shoppers around the fashion area and to advise on locations and bargains.

Most of the streets of the Quadrilatero d'Oro have, interspersed with the shops, a number of *palazzi*. Some, particularly in Via Monte Napoleone, have neo-Classical frontages and porticoed courtyards.

Just to the northeast of the fashion district are the **Giardini Pubblici**, Milan's public gardens. They cover some 17ha (42 acres) and were originally laid out in 1782 by Piermarini, who used the grounds of suppressed monasteries. Within the public gardens are the city's **Planetarium** (open according to the programme with guided tours) and the **Museum of Natural History**, which has a good collection of fossils (including dinosaurs), minerals and insects.

Fashion and Fraud

Anyone strolling around the Quadrilatero d'Oro (Golden Quadrangle) will have little doubt that Milan regards itself as the fashion capital of the world. Not only are there shops with household names such as Versace, Gucci, Armani and Benetton, but the Italians dress in the latest fashion. The Milanese like to *fare bella figura* or cut a fine figure – even the footballers look like male models. Unfortunately the fashion world was caught up in the fraud and corruption allegations of the 1990s, and two of its leading figures have been assassinated – Gianni Versace in Florida and Maurizio Gucci in Milan.

☆ *See* Map C–E4 | ★★

Above: *Palazzo Reale was once the seat of the Visconti family.*

PALAZZO REALE

Situated just to the southeast of the Duomo is the Palazzo Reale, a building with a chequered history. When Milan was a *comune* in the 11th and 12th centuries, the Palazzo was the town hall. In 1598 it was the location of the first theatre in Milan. Later it was the seat of the Visconti family, but when the front part of the building was removed to make way for the cathedral, the Dukes of Milan moved to the Castello Sforzesco (*see* page 18). The palace subsequently became the residence of both the Spanish and Austrian governors. After unification, the building was renamed the Palazzo Reale (Royal Palace). It was handed over to the city authorities in the 20th century.

The second floor of the Palazzo Reale houses the **Civico Museo d'Arte Contemporanea (CIMAC)**, Milan's modern art museum. It has a fine collection of paintings and sculptures, including work by Klee, Picasso, Modigliani and Matisse.

A wing of the Palazzo Reale is occupied by the **Museo del Duomo**. Among its collections are paintings, sculptures, stained-glass windows and a host of religious objects from the cathedral. A star exhibit is a wooden model of the Duomo dating from 1519.

Palazzo Reale
⊠ Piazza del Duomo 12
☎ 02 875 672
⏰ open for exhibitions only
💰 admission charges (amounts vary)
M 1, 3, Duomo
🍴 restaurants nearby

Civico Museo d'Arte Contemporanea
⊠ Piazza del Duomo 12
☎ 02 655 1445
⏰ 10:00–13:00 and 14:30–18:30 Mon, Wed–Fri, 10:30–18:30 Sat–Sun, closed Tue

Museo del Duomo
⊠ Via Arcivescovado 15
☎ 02 860 358
⏰ 09:30–12:30 and 15:00–18:00 Tue–Sun, closed Mon
M Duomo

🧭 See Map C–B4/5	★ ★

NATIONAL MUSEUM OF SCIENCE AND TECHNOLOGY

National Museum of Science and Technology
✉ Via San Vittore 21
☎ 02 485 551
🖥 www.museo scienza.org
🕐 09:30–17:00 Tue– Fri, 09:30–18:30 Sat
💰 admission charges
M 2, Sant'Ambrogio

Just a stone's throw from the Church of Santa Maria delle Grazie is another location for Leonardo da Vinci fans – the National Museum of Science and Technology. It is housed in the 16th-century Monastery of San Vittore, which, after the monasteries were suppressed, became a military hospital and later a barracks. Badly damaged during World War II, the monastery was restored soon afterwards and then became the museum in 1947.

The museum is based around two cloistered courtyards and visitors can see the remains of a Roman fort, revealed after wartime bombing.

The collections occupy a number of buildings, and there are sections dealing with transport, metallurgy, physics, optics, acoustics, printing, cinema, photography and astronomy. The **Leonardo da Vinci Gallery** attracts people by the score and his inventions are well displayed. There is a Leonardo self-portrait engraved on a glass panel, and there is a room dedicated to his drawings and models, some of which can be operated by visitors.

Below: *Engraved self-portrait of Leonardo at the Museo Nazionale della Scienza e della Tecnica.*

Santa Maria Presso San Satiro
✉ Via Torino 17/19
☎ 02 874 683
🕐 Mon–Sat 08:30–11:30, 15:30–17:30; Sun 16:30–17:30
💰 admission free
Ⓜ 1, 3, Duomo

See Map C–E4 | ★ ★

SANTA MARIA PRESSO SAN SATIRO

San Satiro was the little-known brother of San Ambrose. An equally little-known 9th-century archbishop decided that Satiro should be remembered and left money when he died for the building of a church in his name. Little remains today of this 9th-century structure except the Capella della Pietà in the form of a Greek cross.

Donato Bramante was commissioned in 1478 to build the church, initially to house a 13th-century image of the Virgin. The image was said to have bled when attacked by a maniac wielding a knife. Look for the story on the fresco above the high altar.

Bramante found that the space was tight, so he built an exceptionally large barrel-vaulted central nave and then relied on perspective and optical illusions to achieve effect. He created the illusion of an apse (in a space of 97cm/38in) by using trompe

Below: *The Church of Santa Maria Presso San Satiro dates from 876, but owes much of its present appearance to the work of Bramante in the 15th century.*

l'oeil. Note, too, Bramante's octagonal baptistry. The newly restored Capella della Pietà has fragments of early medieval frescoes and a terracotta sculpture of the *Pietà*, probably dating from the late 15th century.

To appreciate the exterior of San Satiro, walk along Via Speronari from where there are good views of the brick-built 11th-century campanile, claimed to be the oldest in Lombardy, and the Renaissance/Baroque rear façade completed in 1871.

SAN SATIRO & AMBROSIANA

See Map C–D4/E4 ★★

AMBROSIANA

On Piazza Pio XI, just west of the Duomo, the Ambrosiana is a huge library and art gallery set up in 1603 by Cardinal Federico Borromeo, cousin of the better-known bishop. It was designed as a comprehensive cultural centre, including an art school (opened in 1629) and a library (dating from 1609). Federico Borromeo donated his personal collection of 172 paintings to the centre and this forms the basis of the displays today. These include Titian's *Adoration of the Magi*, Caravaggio's basket of worm-eaten fruit (thought to be the first still life painted in Italy) and Bassano's *Rest on the Flight from Egypt*.

Paintings from outside Borromeo's collection include Leonardo's *Musician* and Botticelli's *Madonna del Padiglione*. Among later works on the upper floors are a self-portrait of the sculptor Antonio Canova and two paintings by Tiepolo. Don't miss the somewhat chaotic Galbiati wing and the Museo Settala which display a hodgepodge of fossils, scientific instruments, minerals and oddities such as the gloves that Napoleon wore when he met his Nemesis at Waterloo.

The Library, which is well used by researchers and academics (a letter of introduction is required), contains over 750,000 books and priceless manuscripts, including some of Leonardo's sketchbooks.

Above: *The rather severe façade of the Pinacoteca Ambrosiana. Among the paintings to be seen here is the original collection of Cardinal Federico Borromeo, cousin of San Carlo.*

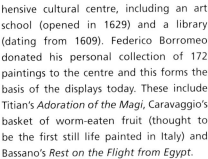

Ambrosiana
✉ Piazza Pio XI 2
☎ 02 806 921
🖳 www.ambrosiana.it
🕒 library 09:30–17:00 Mon–Fri; art gallery 10:00–17:30 Tue–Sun
♿ admission charge
M 1, 3, Duomo; 1, Cordusio

See Map C–D5 | ★★

Above: *The interior of the Basilica of San Lorenzo Maggiore.*
Opposite: *Once Milan's rather seedy port district, the Navigli is now one of the liveliest quarters of the city, with festivals, shops, markets and many restaurants.*

Basilica of San Lorenzo Maggiore
✉ Corso di Porta Ticinese 39
☎ 02 8940 4129
🕑 Mon–Sat 07:30–12:30, 14:30–18:30; Sun 07:30–18:00
M 3, Missori

BASILICA OF SAN LORENZO MAGGIORE

The basilica, sometimes called San Lorenzo alle Colonne, is located just to the south of the city centre near the old Porta Ticinese gateway. In front of the church are 16 Corinthian columns dating from the 2nd or 3rd century, originally belonging to an unidentified temple.

San Lorenzo is Milan's oldest church, dating back to the 4th century, and its design is unlike any work of the Lombard architects. It suffered as a result of many fires during the 12th and 13th centuries, being rebuilt on the original Roman model. After the dome collapsed in 1573, the church was redesigned. The large and rather gloomy interior of San Lorenzo is built in a circular pattern with an ambulatory and a matroneum (women's gallery). On either side of the main altar are two huge arches with, unusually, their columns upside down – symbolism meant to show Christianity rising from the depths of paganism.

Be sure not to miss the superb 5th-century octagonal Cappella di Sant'Aquilino, which some authorities claim to have been an imperial mausoleum – supported by the evidence of 4th-century mosaics, a 3rd-century sarcophagus and a Roman portal. Further Roman relics can be seen in the passage behind the high altar.

🌼 See Map B–A4	★★

THE NAVIGLI

To the southwest of the city centre are the remains of a once extensive canal system. First constructed in the 12th century, the canals linked Milan with the network of north Italian waterways. The canals brought Canoglia marble to the city to build the Duomo, along with fruit and vegetables from the countryside plus coal and salt from the ports. In the opposite direction went handmade goods such as textiles. Many of the canals were filled in during the 1930s, but it is interesting to note that Milan was Italy's 10th largest port as late as the 1950s.

The area around the canals was once a staunch working-class area and it is still possible to see the old wash houses, the Vicolo dei Lavandai, that lined the canals. Today, however, the area has been gentrified. Real estate values have jumped and the old blocks of flats now command high prices, while bou- tiques and antique shops line the water- front. The Navigli area also claims to have the trendiest restaurants in Milan. A popular antique market is held on the canal side on the last Sunday of every month in summer, and there is also a flea market each Saturday.

Milan's Astounding Population Growth

The earliest population figures available show that from the 13th to 15th centuries Milan had a population of around 200,000, making it the largest city in Europe. During the 1630 plague the figure dropped to 60,000. Thereafter there was a gradual recovery until the end of the 19th century when there was a mas- sive spurt in population numbers. By 1923 it had reached 850,000, and after World War II it neared 1,400,000, making Milan the second largest city in Italy and 10th largest in Europe. Greater Milan today has 3,780,000 inhabitants including migrants from southern Italy and other parts of the world such as North Africa and Asia.

Stazione Centrale
✉ Piazzale Duca d'Aosta
M 2, 3, Centrale
🍴 restaurants nearby

☆ *See* Map B–B3 | ★

STAZIONE CENTRALE

Milan's main station was designed by Ulisse Stacchini and work began in 1912. Progress was slow, however, and the building was not completed until 1931. It defies architectural definition (the Liberty style is perhaps the closest) and is really a political and ideological statement, reflecting Mussolini's obsession with making the trains run on time. Faced with light grey Aurisina stone, it is embellished with a forest of Corinthian columns, statues, murals and relief sculpture, while the roof is topped with winged horses. The façade alone is 207m (679ft) wide, and 36m (118ft) high.

Inside the station an imposing flight of steps leads up to a concourse with a booking office, shops (some open 24 hours) and a tourist information office. Here are four massive mosaic murals representing Milan and the destinations of Rome, Florence and Turin. The numerous platforms are covered with a spectacular glass and iron barrel roof.

As well as routes within Lombardy, the Stazione Centrale handles international trains such as Eurostar. Shuttle buses run from Malpensar Airport to the station, but note that trains from the airport stop at Cadorna Metro station rather than Centrale.

Milan's other train stations are **Stazione Porta Garibaldi** in Piazza Freud and **Stazione di Cadorna (Milano Nord)** in Piazzale Cadorna.

Below: *Stazione Centrale, Milan's main railway station, has an impressive façade built in the time of Mussolini.*

☆ *See Map C–D6* | ★

SANT'EUSTORGIO

Some distance to the south of the historic centre and close to the *navigli* (canals, see page 29), Sant' Eustorgio was built in the 11th century to house the relics of the Magi, which were taken to Milan by Bishop Eustorgius. In 1162, Frederick Barbarossa destroyed the building and took the relics to Cologne (they were not returned

until 1903). The church was rebuilt in 1190, with the addition of a bell tower topped with a cone-shaped cusp. This is Milan's tallest bell tower and the first to have a clock. The simple façade gives little indication of the delights of the interior, which has so many art treasures it is almost like a museum. Not to be missed is the Portinari Chapel, which was originally commissioned by a Milanese banker. In the entrance is the magnificently carved raised tomb of St Peter the Martyr, built by Giovanni di Balduccio and dating from the mid-14th century. The other joy of the chapel is in the frescoes by Vincenzo Foppa that adorn the walls and ceiling. They were not discovered until 1878 when building work was taking place. Most of the artworks can be seen in the string of chapels of varying ages on the south side of the church.

Above: *The façade of Sant'Eustorgio is neo-Romanesque in style and mainly brick-built.*

Sant'Eustorgio
✉ Piazza Sant'
Eustorgio 1
☎ 02 5810 1583
🕘 07:30–12:00 and
15:30–18:30
💰 admission free
M 2, Stazione Genova
🍽 restaurants nearby

See Map B–A3 | ★

Above: *The futuristic San Siro stadium, home of Milan's two famous football clubs, Inter and AC.*

SAN SIRO STADIUM

The stadium is located in the San Siro neighbourhood with its wide open spaces and luxury apartment blocks. It is now officially known as the Meazza after Giuseppe Meazza, a highly regarded footballer who played for both Milan's teams – Inter and AC. Originally built in 1926, the stadium was modernized in the 1950s and again in 1990 when a roof and a third tier were added, giving it a seating capacity of 85,000. Although the third-tier seats look fairly remote from the pitch, there is no athletics track surrounding the pitch, so the fans are close to the action.

The AC Milan club was actually founded by a group of English and other foreign expats but when the Italian Football Federation decided to ban foreign players, the internationals from the AC club decided to form an international club, which became known as Internazionale or, as it is known today, Inter. Some world-renowned players have performed for the two clubs over the years and memorabilia and silverware can be seen in the **Museo Inter e Milan** to be found within the stadium. The museum is open on match days until 30 minutes before kick-off. Tours of the stadium can also be arranged.

San Siro acts as a concert venue where Italian and international acts perform.

Violence on the Terraces

The 'English Disease' of football hooliganism seems to have spread to the Italian *liga*, particularly when it comes to local 'derbys' between Inter and AC Milan. The *Milanesi* fanatically support one team or the other and violence has often erupted on the terraces, with fighting and coins and other items being thrown onto the pitch. In a recent match flares were directed at the players by supporters of the losing team, with the result that the match was abandoned and points deducted from the clubs.

See Map D–C5 ★

CERTOSA DI PAVIA

The Certosa or Charterhouse, 10km (6 miles) north of Pavia, is reached by bus or train from Milan. It was built by Gian Galeazzo Visconti in the 1390s as a family mausoleum. Architects and masons working on Milan's cathedral also spent time on the Certosa, but the main input was from Giovanni Antonio Amadeo, who was responsible for the façade. The building shows a transition in styles from Gothic to Renaissance and is considered to be the most important monument in Lombardy after Milan's Duomo.

Cistercian monks took over in 1968. They maintain the old traditions, including a vow of silence; a few of the monks are released from this vow to take guided tours around the Certosa. A highlight of the tour is the façade of the church, with over 70 statues of saints and prophets. The interior has groin vaulting, a huge metalwork screen, marble mosaics on the floors, and stained-glass windows. In the north transept is the tomb of Ludovici el Moro and his wife Beatrice d'Este (by Cristoforo Solari) and the south transept has the tomb of Gian Galeazzo Visconti. The Little Cloister leads to the arcaded Great Cloister, with 122 arches supported by marble columns. The cloister is surrounded by the monks' comfortable cells – each has its own bedroom, study, chapel and walled garden. The refectory has ceiling frescoes by Bergognone and an elaborately carved pulpit.

San Siro Stadium
✉ via Piccolomini 5
☎ stadium 02 4870 7123, museum (Gate 21) 02 404 2432
🕑 Mon–Sat 10:00–17:00, match days 30 minutes before kick-off
M 1, Lotto

Certosa di Pavia
✉ via del Monumento 5
☎ 0382 925 613
🕑 09:00–11:30 and 14:30–17:30 Tue–Sun; closing times may vary in summer and winter

Below: *The façade of the Certosa di Pavia, attributed to Giovanni Antonio Amadeo.*

Above: *One of the artworks at San Maurizio, many of which were painted by Bernardino Luini, a follower of Leonardo da Vinci.*

Opposite: *A nude statue of Napoleon in the centre of the courtyard of the Pinacoteca di Brera, attributed to Canova.*

Places of Worship

San Maurizio

The church of San Maurizio was begun in 1503 for a closed order of Benedictine nuns, and the design of the building made provision for strict divisions between the public and the nuns. The exterior of the church is of little interest, but the interior has some superb frescoes attributed to Leonardo da Vinci's follower Bernardino Luini. They have been dated at around 1530 and are probably the artist's last work. In one of the chapels Luini painted scenes from the life of St Catherine, including the *Decapitation of St Catherine*. It is believed that the face of the saint is actually a portrait of Countess Bianca Maria di Challant, who was herself beheaded in the courtyard of the Castello Sforzesco in 1516.

✉ *Corso Magenta 15*
☎ *02 866 660*
🕐 *07:30–12:00 and 16:00–17:30 Tue–Sun*
M *1, 2, Cadorna*

San Fedele

San Fedele is the Milan headquarters of the Jesuits. It is Baroque in style with a single nave. It dates from 1569, although the choir crypt and cupola are a century later. Of interest is the fact that the choir stalls were taken from the church of Santa Maria della Scala when it was demolished to make way for the opera house.

✉ *Piazza San Fedele*
☎ *02 7200 8027*
🖥 *www.gesuiti.it*
🕐 *daily 07:30–14:30*
and 16:00–19:00
♿ *admission free*
M *Duomo*

San Marco

San Marco was built by the Augustinians in 1254 on the site of an earlier church. The façade was rebuilt in the 1870s by Carlo Maciachini in neo-Gothic style. The numerous chapels have some interesting paintings, mainly in the Lombard style.

✉ *Piazza San Marco 2*
☎ *02 2900 2598*
🕐 *daily 07:30–12:00*
and 16:00–19:00
♿ *admission free*
M *Lanza*

San Nazaro Maggiore

Built between 382 and 386 on the instructions of St Ambrose, it is claimed to be the first church to be built in the shape of a cross. San Nazaro's remains are in a silver vessel in the choir. The church was largely destroyed by fire in 1075 but swiftly rebuilt. An octagonal chapel was added in the 16th century as a mausoleum for a wealthy family and much of the neo-Classical interior dates from the 1830s. Much damage was suffered during World War II.

✉ *Piazza San Nazaro*
☎ *02 5830 7719*
🕐 *daily 07:30–12:00*
and 15:00–18:30
♿ *admission free*
M *Missori*

More places of worship on pages 14, 17, 21, 26, 28 and 31.

The Emperor Without his Clothes

Dominating the cobbled courtyard of the Brera Art Gallery (see page 22) is a bronze statue of Napoleon. This is fitting, as the Emperor was responsible for setting up the gallery. However, this is no ordinary statue of Napoleon – it is a nude Napoleon! Antonio Canova's bronze statue was executed in 1809. The emperor was middle-aged when he conquered Milan and he is depicted here as a nude young god, holding a sceptre in his right hand and a personification of victory in his left hand.

One of Milan's most famous residents, Manzoni wrote what is seen as Italy's greatest novel, *I Promessi Sposi* (The Betrothed), describing life in Milan in the 17th century. He used a form of Italian that everyone could understand, stirring feelings for unification. His former home, Casa Manzoni, in Via Morone, is now a museum and the seat of the National Centre for Manzoni Studies. The museum also houses the Lombard History Society's collection of over 40,000 books.

Opposite: *Ca' Grande's Cortile Maggiore is decorated with busts sculpted in Angera stone from Lake Maggiore.*
Below: *A weeping willow tree graces the main courtyard of Ca' Grande.*

Museums and Galleries
Ca' Grande

Southeast of the Duomo is the Casa Grande or Ospedale Maggiore. This former hospital was built in the mid-15th century for Francesco Sforza, who planned to centralize the city's many hospitals. It has a magnificent arcaded central courtyard, which separated the men's and women's quarters. Since 1952 Ca' Grande has been the home of the Liberal Arts faculty of Milan's State University. Ca' Grande's 17th-century Church of the Annunciata is located in the courtyard and is open to visitors during the university term time.

✉ via Festa del Perdono 7
🕐 Mon–Fri 09:00–17:00, Sat 08:00–23:30
M Duomo, Missori

Museo Poldi Pezzoli

This museum is only a short walk from the Piazza della Scala. As well as some highly regarded artwork, including paintings by Bellini, Mantegna and Canaletto, there are also displays of glassware, clocks, porcelain and tapestry.
✉ Via Manzoni 12
☎ 02 794 889
🖥 www.museopoldi pezzoli.it
🕐 09:30–12:30 and 14:20–18:00 Tue–Sat, 09:30–12:30 Sun
M 3, Montenapoleone

Museo Archeologico

Based in a former monastery, the archaeological museum has some interesting collections from prehistoric, Etruscan and Roman times. Highlights are a model of Roman

Milan, a bust of Hercules and the Coppa Trivulzio, a superb relic of Roman glass-making.

⊠ corso Magenta 15
☎ 02 8645 0011
⊕ 09:30–17:30 Tue–Sun
M 1, 2, Cadorna

Pusterla di Sant'Ambrogio

Set in one of the medieval city gates, this museum has a collection of ancient weapons and criminological artefacts. The gate itself is a 1939 copy of the medieval original.

⊠ via Carducci 41
☎ 02 805 3505
⊕ 10:00–13:00 and 15:00–19:00 Tue–Sun
M 3, Duomo

Museo Bagatti Valsecchi

Located in the former house of the two Bagatti Valsecchi brothers, the collection in this museum gives a good indication of the tastes in art and furniture in the late 19th century.

The rooms are devoted to tapestries, ivory work and paintings, along with a superb collection of furniture that children would have used in the 15th to 17th centuries.

⊠ via Santo Spirito 10
☎ 02 7600 6132
🖥 www.museobagatti valsecchi.org
⊕ 10:00–18:00 Tue–Sun
M 3, Montenapoleone

Museo del Risorgimento

Set in the Palazzo Moriggia in the Brera district, this museum covers the course of the unification movement from the 1700s to 1870. Amongst the memorabilia are the clothes worn by Napoleon at his coronation in Milan, the black hats with plumes worn by leading members of the revolt, and also political leaflets from the time.

⊠ via Borgonuovo 23
☎ 02 8846 4176
⊕ 09:00–18:00 Tue–Sun
M 3, Montenapoleone

The Amateur Bishop

Ambrose (Ambrogio) was a Roman governor sent to Milan in 374 to oversee the election of a new bishop. This was at a time of some theological turmoil, following the Arian controversy. Ambrose made an eloquent speech calming the crowds, who suddenly took up the chant 'Ambrose Bishop'. Although he had not even been baptized, he converted to Christianity immediately and in just over a week he had been made Bishop of Milan. He proved to be extremely successful at preserving the unity of the Church and establishing good relations between the Church and the Empire. Such was the reputation of this amateur bishop that he became the patron saint of Milan, and people from the city are still known today as Ambrosiani.

Opposite: *The Arco della Pace was built as a triumphal arch for Napoleon, but was later dedicated to peace.*

Museo di Milano

Located in an old palace, the Museum of Milan concentrates specifically on paintings with relevance to the history of Milan, giving a particularly good indication of life during the Napoleonic era. Other interesting items, such as porcelain, sculptures and furniture, were donated by the Countess Bolognini, the former owner of the palazzo.

⊠ *Palazzo Morando Attendolo Bolognini, via Sant'Andrea 6*
☎ *02 7600 6245*
💻 *www.museidel centro.mi.it*
🕑 *Tue–Sun 14:00–17:30*
💰 *admission free*
Ⓜ *San Bibila, Montenapoleone*

Museo Civico di Storia Naturale

Situated within the Giardini Pubblici (see page 40), this is Milan's oldest museum, and the exhibits, mainly of skeletons, rocks and fossils, appear to be similarly dated. The full-size dinosaur skeleton on display will certainly appeal to children.

⊠ *Corsa Venezia 55*
☎ *02 8846 3280*
🕑 *daily 09:00–18:00, Sat–Sun 09:00–18:30*
Ⓜ *Porta Venezia, Palestro*

Museo del Cinema

To be found on the western edge of the Giardini Pubblici, housed in a 17th-century palazzo, this museum is an absolute delight for film buffs. On show is equipment and posters from the early days of film. Clips from Italian film classics are shown regularly.

⊠ *Giardini Pubblici, via D. Manin 2*
☎ *02 655 4977*
💰 *admission charged*
🕑 *15:00–18:00 daily*
Ⓜ *Porta Venezia, Palestro*

More museums and galleries on pages 16, 19, 21, 22, 23, 24, 25 and 27.

Monuments
Statue of Victor Emmanuel II

This huge bronze equestrian statue of Victor Emmanuel, which was unveiled in 1896, is the work of Ercole Rosa. The statue depicts the king at the Battle of San Martino in 1859, while the sides of the massive plinth show the triumphant entry of the Piedmont troops into Milan after the Battle of Magenta (1859).

✉ *at the western end of the Piazza del Duomo*

Monument to Leonardo da Vinci

Pietro Magni's monument to da Vinci was erected in 1872. On the corners of the plinth are some of Leonardo's pupils: Boltraffio, Salaino, Oggiono and da Sesto. Between their figures are reliefs showing the various fields of work in which Leonardo excelled – anatomy, hydraulic engineering, painting and architecture. (*See* the picture on page 46.)

✉ *in the centre of Piazza della Scala*

Arco della Pace

Standing 25m (82ft) high, the construction of this triumphal arch began in 1807 in celebration of Napoleon's victories. On Napoleon's fall from power, work stopped on the arch and it was not resumed until 1826, when Francis I of Austria dedicated it to Peace.

✉ *at the far end of Parco Sempione*

Saint or Sinner?

When **Napoleon** marched into Milan, the city welcomed him with open arms. Eighteen years later, the Milanese had had enough and were glad to see the back of him. To his credit, he had established Milan as the capital of the Cisalpine Republic, inaugurated extensive public works, reformed the education and legal systems, and founded Milan's Fine Arts Academy and the Brera Museum and Gallery. On the other hand, his administration imposed high taxes and plundered art treasures from churches and private collections. Perhaps Napoleon's most lasting memorial is that he put into many people's minds the potential for a single, unified Italian state.

Parks and Open Spaces

For a city of its size, Milan has relatively few parks and green areas. The central part of the city has only two open spaces, **Parco Sempione**, once the hunting grounds of the Sforza family, and **Giardini Pubblici**, the main civic park. Both areas cater well for children, with roundabouts, mini-trains and play areas. Further afield, water-sports buffs could head for the **Idropark Fila**, a former seaplane runway close to Linate Airport, which boasts swimming, water skiing, rowing and, in winter, an ice rink.

Below: *Parco Sempione is designed in typically English style, with lakes and shady trees.*

Green Spaces
Parco Sempione

This park, once the Sforza family's hunting grounds, was remodelled in the late 19th century by Emilio Alemagna in what was considered to be typically English style. Today, the park covers about 47ha (116 acres) and includes a number of lakes between the mature trees. Almost hidden among this leafiness is the Monument to Napoleon III, dating from 1881 and brought here in 1927 from its original site at the Senate building.

☒ *Castello Sforzesco*

☉ *daily 06:30 to dusk*

M *Cairoli, Cadorna, Lanza*

Giardini Pubblici

These gardens form the largest public park in Milan. They were designed by Giuseppe Piermarini in 1784 and enlarged in the following century. There are lakes, waterfalls, specimen trees and jogging tracks along with a couple of pleasant bars. Within the gardens are the zoo, planetarium, Palazzo Dugnani and Museo di Storia Naturale. Around the park are more museums and art galleries.

☒ *Bastioni di Porta Venezia*

☉ *daily 06:30 to sunset*

M *Palestro, Porta Venezia*

ACTIVITIES
Sport and Recreation

The Milanese are passionate about sport. For many it will be simply spectator sports such as soccer at San Siro, horse racing at the nearby Ippodrome or watching car and motorbike racing at

Monza. For the younger and wealthier set, however, active sport is important. There are several private **golf** courses around the outskirts of Milan, but only one public course – Golf le Revedine, 7km (4.5 miles) outside the city, tel: 02 5760 6420. **Tennis** is also popular, but for the workaholic Milanese **squash** is a quicker and cheaper fix. Professional **cycling** has always had a big following in northern Italy and many people cycle for leisure. There are many cycle paths running through the centre of Milan, mostly following the towpaths of the canals. **Swimming** is an attractive proposition, particularly in the summer. Two recommended public pools are Parco Solari, tel: 02 469 5278, and Piscina Cozzi, tel: 02 659 9703. Visitors using swimming pools in Milan should be aware that bathing caps (for both sexes) are obligatory.

The lakes north of Milan provide venues for a wealth of recreational activities. There is a long **skiing** season in the Alps, while in summer the mountains are popular for hiking and rock climbing. The lakes are used for a variety of water sports. The northern end of Lake Garda is one of the world's

Above: *Outdoor chess on a Sunday morning is a gentle form of recreation that many northern Italians enjoy.*

Staying in Good Shape

The Milanese have always put a high value on looking smart and wearing the coolest clothes. In recent years they have also realized the worth of being in good shape physically, hence the phenomenal growth of leisure clubs and gyms in the city. Here will be found all the latest technical equipment to produce a trim figure, along with sunbeds, aerobics studios, squash courts and pools. All good health and leisure clubs, needless to say, will have a shop to sell the obligatory designer-wear lycra.

Above: *Funereal monuments to the great and good of Milan can be seen at the Cimitero Monumentale, which has, strangely, become one of the city's tourist attractions.*

prime **windsurfing** locations and also provides challenging **sailing** conditions. **Canoeing** has boomed in recent years, particularly on the white-water stretches of the rivers leading into the lakes.

Alternative Milan

It is hard to think of a cemetery as a tourist attraction, but the **Cimitero Monumentale** is just that. It is the burial ground of the great and good of Milan, each trying to outdo the other with the magnificence of their funerary monuments, hiring only the best sculptors for the task.

The cemetery was begun in 1866 and the monuments are largely Art Nouveau in style, although there are some notable modern forms. The monuments include a pyramid, a life-size crucifixion and a sculpted recreation of *The Last Supper*.

The central focus of the complex is a huge neo-Gothic temple, known as the Temple of Fame, containing the tomb of the writer Alessandro Manzoni, as well as those of Luca Beltrami and Arturo Toscanini, plus busts of Verdi and the unification figures Cavour and Garibaldi.

It is interesting to note that the non-Catholics are buried in a separate area. The office at the entrance to the cemetery provides a map showing the whereabouts of the most interesting monuments. The *Cimitero* is a long way from a Metro station so you will need a taxi or bus to get there, but don't miss it.

Using the Metro

Using Milan's underground railway system or metro could not be simpler. Maps of the metro show that there are three lines – Line 1 coloured red, Line 2 coloured green and Line 3 coloured yellow (plus the Passante high-speed link, coloured blue). Cheap tickets can be bought from newsstands and tobacconists and are valid for 75 minutes, anywhere on the system. Trains are generally clean and safe and you can reach 90 per cent of the places mentioned in this book by using the metro.

Walking Tours
Walking Tour 1

Start your tour at the western end of the **Piazza del Duomo**, next to the bronze equestrian **Statue of Victor Emanuele II**, the work of Ercole Rosa, which was unveiled in 1896. The statue depicts the king at the Battle of San Martino in 1859, while the sides of the massive plinth show the triumphal entry of the Piedmont troops into Milan after the Battle of Magenta (1859). Look towards the stunning west front of the **Duomo** (see page 14), with its marble stone and superb array of statues. After touring the Duomo, proceed around the north side to take the lift to its roof, giving panoramic views across the city.

Returning to street level, walk across the front of the Duomo to the **Palazzo Reale** (see page 24), with a choice of two museums. On one wing of the ground floor is the **Museo del Duomo**, which houses artefacts from the history of the cathedral, while **Civico Museo d'Arte Contemporanea (CIMAC)** on the second floor contains the city's modern art collection.

Leaving the Palazzo Reale, walk behind the east end of the Duomo and into Corso Vittorio Emanuele II. Follow this avenue until you reach **Piazza San Babila**. This square was renovated during the fascist era and provides an interesting contrast between

> **Cimitero Monumentale**
> ✉ Piazzale Cimitero Monumentale
> ☎ 02 8846 5600
> 💰 admission free
> 🕐 08:30–17:15 Tue–Sun, closed pm during holidays

> **Walking Tour 1**
> **Location:** Map C–E4/F4
> **Distance:** about 3km (1.9 miles)
> **Duration:** about 2 hours, not counting visits
> **Start:** Piazza del Duomo
> **Finish:** Piazza del Duomo

Below: *The equestrian statue of Victor Emanuel II in the bustling Piazza del Duomo.*

ACTIVITIES

Walking Tours
Much of the historic core of Milan can be covered on foot, without recourse to the Metro or taxis. In the height of the hot and humid Italian summer it is probably best to take the walks in the early morning or late afternoon, which would give the opportunity for a long lunch. The walks are designed to take in a cross section of interests, with churches, museums, art galleries and shopping opportunities. Both walks start and end at the Piazza del Duomo.

the Torre di Corso Matteotti, Milan's first high-rise building, and the attractive Romanesque Church of San Babila, which dates back to the 11th century.

From Piazza San Babila, turn left into Corso Matteotti and then almost immediately right into Via Monte Napoleone. You are now approaching the **Quadrilatero d'Oro** (see page 23), Milan's famous fashion district. Turn right into Via Sant'Andrea, left along Via Della Spiga and then left again along Via Gesu, and you will return to Via Monte Napoleone, completing the fashion rectangle, passing such stores as Versace, Prada, Armani and Dolce & Gabbana. Non-shopoholics could instead visit two museums. On Via Sant'Andrea is the **Museo di Milano** (see page 38), while on Via Gesu is the **Museo Bagatti Valsecchhi** (see page 37), containing a comprehensive collection of Italian Renaissance art.

Continue northwest along Via Monte Napoleone, which becomes Via Crocce Rosa and then Via Borgonuovo. This is now the **Brera quarter**. On the left is the **Museo del Risorgimento** (see page 37), which charts

the rise of the Risorgimento movement that eventually led to the unification of Italy. Exiting the museum, turn left into Via Fiori Oscuri and left again into Via Brera. On the left is the **Pinacoteca di Brera** (see page 22), the city's foremost art gallery. Note in the courtyard the nude Statue of Napoleon (see page 35).

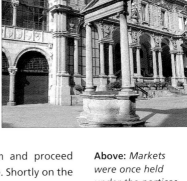

Continue south along Via Brera, turning left at the crossroads into via Monte di Pieta. Take the first right into Via Romagnosi. At the crossroads with Via Manzoni is the **Museo Poldi Pezzoli** (*see* page 36), housing the art collection of Poldi Pezzoli, a rich Milanese banker. Leave the museum and proceed southeast along Via Morone. Shortly on the right is the **Casa del Manzoni**, which was the home of the well-known Milanese writer Alessandro Manzoni. A tour of the building shows, amongst other things, his study, where he wrote his novel *I Promesi Sposi*. Return now to the Piazza del Duomo via Piazza Meda and Via San Paolo.

Walking Tour 2

Leave Piazza del Duomo from the less attractive southwest side of the square along Via Turino. Almost immediately on the left is the **Church of Santa Maria Presso San Satiro** (*see* page 26), a gem of Lombard Renaissance architecture. Don't miss the trompe l'oeil choir, the work of Bramante. From here take the first right along Via Asole. Ahead is the **Pinacoteca Ambrosiana** (*see* page 27), a palace specially built by Federico Borromeo in the early 17th century to house Milan's first library and academy of painting. From the Pinacoteca, cross Piazza Pio XI and walk along Via Cantu, reaching at the end **Piazza Mercanti**. This market square dates back to medieval times, when lawyers worked under the

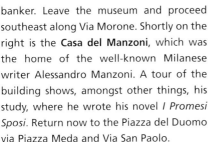

Above: *Markets were once held under the porticos of Piazza Mercanti, which was also the site of a prison and the law courts.*
Opposite: *Casa Manzoni, the house where the author Alessandro Manzoni lived from 1814 till his death in 1873.*

Walking Tour 2
Location: Map C–E4/E3
Distance: 1.2km (¾ mile)
Duration: about 1 hour, excluding stops
Start: Piazza del Duomo
Finish: Piazza del Duomo

Above: *The Statue of Leonardo with his four pupils dominates the Piazza della Scala.*
Opposite: *Milan's trams, which are frequent but often crowded, form part of an efficient public transport system.*

porticos. Impressive buildings are the 13th-century Palazzo della Ragione and the Loggia degli Osli. Note, too, the quaint 15th-century well in the centre of the piazza.

From Piazza Mercanti head northwest towards Piazza Cordusio. Cross the square and go past the Cordusio Metro station to reach Via Grossi. Follow this road to the right, which leads into Via Santa Margherita. In a short distance you arrive at **Piazza della Scala**. In the centre of the square is Pietro Magni's Statue of Leonardo da Vinci, erected in 1872. On the corners of the plinth are da Vinci's pupils Boltraffio, Salaino, Oggiono and da Sesto. Between their figures are reliefs showing the various fields of work in which Leonardo excelled – anatomy, architecture, hydraulic engineering and painting. On the southwest side of the square is the 16th-century **Palazzo Marino**, now the City Hall. On the opposite side is the world-famous opera house, **La Scala** (*see* page 16). If you cannot go to a performance, take in a guided tour of the building to soak up the atmosphere. Don't miss La Scala's **museum**, which has a fascinating collection of opera memorobilia. From the Piazza della Scala, head into the fashionable **Galleria Vittorio Emanuele II** (*see* page 20), an opportunity for shopping and window gazing. Emerge from the Galleria back into the Piazza del Duomo, where a welcoming drink awaits at one of the many bars and restaurants.

Organized Tours

Joining an organized tour is a convenient, and fairly cheap way of getting an overview of Milan before homing in on places of particular interest. The city's main tourist office, the **Azienda di Promozione Turistica (APT)**, provides information about tours and tour operators (as well as free maps, hotel lists and information on cultural events).

A guided bus tour is provided by **Autostradale**. Buses leave from outside the APT office in the Piazza del Duomo at 09:30 Tue–Sun, visiting the Cimitero Monumentale, Castello Sforzesco and the Church of Santa Maria delle Grazie among others. The tour lasts three hours and tickets can be booked at the APT. Children under 12 go free. Note that the tour does not operate during the last two weeks in August. The cost of a ticket might seem high, but it includes entry to see Leonardo's *Last Supper*.

Another good option is the **Tram Turistica (or Ciao Milan Tourist Tram)**. Old trams from the 1920s have been converted for tourists, with headphones and multilingual

Tourist Information Centres
Azienda di Promozione Turistica (APT) Milan:
⊠ via Marconi 1, at the side of the Duomo
☎ 02 7252 4301
✆ 02 7252 4350
▭ www.milan infotourist.com
⏱ 08:30–20:00 Mon–Fri, 09:00–13:00 and 14:00–19:00 Sat, 09:00–13:00 and 14:00–17:00 Sun

APT Cremona:
⊠ Piazza del Comune, opposite the Duomo
☎ 0372 23233
⏱ 09:00–12:00 and 15:00–18:00 Mon–Sat, 09:45–12:00 Sun
▭ www.cremona turismo.com

APT Mantua:
⊠ piazza Mantegna 6
☎ 0376 328 253

APT Bergamo:
⊠ viale Vittorio Emanuele II 20
☎ 035 210 204
▭ www.apt.bergamo.it
⏱ 09:00–12:30 and 14:00–17:30 Mon–Fri

APT Bergamo Alta:
⊠ vicolo Aquila Nera 2, off the Piazza Vecchia
☎ 035 232 226
⏱ all year round

APT Pavia:
⊠ via F. Filzi 2
☎ 0382 22156
⏱ 08:30–12:30 and 14:00–18:00 Mon–Sat

Organized Tours
Autostradale
☎ 02 3391 0794
🖥 www.autostradale.it

Ciao Milan Tourist Tram
☎ 02 7200 2584
🖥 www.autostradale.it

Hello Milano
☎ 02 2952 0570

A Friend in Milan
☎ 348 600 6298
🖥 www.friendinmilan.co.uk

Centro Guide Milano
✉ via Marconi 1
☎ 02 2952 0570
🖥 www.centroguidemilano.org
Non profit making company

Sophisticated Italy
☎ 02 4819 6675
🖥 www.sophisticateditaly.com

Opera d'Arte
☎ 02 6900 0579
🖥 www.operadartemilano.it

commentaries. You can jump on and off at a number of locations along the route, including Piazza Castello, Via Alessandro Manzoni (convenient for the fashion area), Santa Maria delle Grazie (for Leonardo's *Last Supper*), Porta Venezia, Via Turino (for Piazza del Duomo) and Piazza Repubblica.

Personalized tours are offered by a number of firms, including **A Friend in Milan** and **Hello Milano**, while **Opera d'Arte** provides individual tours of churches, galleries and museums. Other companies provide car tours, or a shopping companion/guide to the fashion district. With personalized tours, the customer can generally set the itinerary and negotiate a price. Other companies, such as **Sophisticated Italy**, offer small group tours for topics such as gardens, food and drink, and golf.

Fun for Children

Surprisingly, for a city geared to finance and big business, Milan has much to offer children. Infants are welcome in restaurants, where pint-sized meals can usually be rustled up. Many museums cater for children, with the **Museo Nazionale della Scienza e della Technica** (*see* page 25) excelling. As well as the Leonardo inventions there are many hands-on opportunities for young people of all ages. The **Teatro delle Marionette** (tel: 02 469 4440) is Milan's oldest established puppet theatre, with Italian versions of *Punch and Judy* sure to please. The **Museo del Giocattolo e del Bambini** (tel: 02 2641 1585) is geared for children and its attractions include antique toys and a mock-up of a 19th-century classroom. The ever-popular dinosaurs are

FUN FOR CHILDREN

on show at the **Museo Civico di Storia Naturale** (*see* page 38).

Elsewhere in the city, most children will be impressed with the views from the roof of the **Duomo** (*see* page 14) and the little ones will certainly want to feed the pigeons in the piazza below. Even the **Quadrilatero d'Oro** (*see* page 23) has its attractions, with many of the shops providing

designer labels especially for children. The public parks and gardens, particularly the **Giardini Pubblici** (*see* page 40), provide merry-go-rounds and other attractions for young children. Parents with small children should buy a copy of *Milano dei Bambini e delle Mamme* (Milan for Children and Mothers), which lists crèches, babysitting services and places to take kids.

Teenagers would appreciate a visit to a soccer match at **San Siro Stadium** (*see* page 32) or even motor racing at nearby **Monza**. Parents able to take their children further afield could aim for **Gardaland**, a theme park close to the shore of Lake Garda, approximately 80km (50 miles) east of Milan. Opened in 1975, it covers a vast area and has some 38 attractions including an exciting roller coaster, a dolphin pool, Jungle Rapids, a simulation of the Valley of the Kings, and a Blue Tornado that gives the opportunity to take the controls of this American fighter plane.

Above: *One of the many rides at the Gardaland Theme Park on the shores of Lake Garda.*

A Child-friendly Country

Do not worry about taking babies or young children to Milan and its surrounding areas, as they will be made very welcome. Children keep late nights and are not excluded from any family activities. Waiters traditionally make a huge fuss of small children who come to their restaurants and will prepare special portions for them. Older children will find plenty to occupy themselves with and will enjoy the theme parks and boat trips.

Above: *The Galleria Vittorio Emanuele II, forerunner of the indoor shopping mall.* **Opposite:** *Even the most discerning shopper will find plenty of interest in central Milan.*

Shopoholic's Delight
Milan is the undisputed shopping capital of Italy, if not the whole of Europe. It is the home of the world's foremost fashion designers, such as Versace, Armani and Donatella. It then follows that accessories, jewellery and shoes support the designer clothes. Milan is also a world centre of household and furniture design. What Milan displays today, the world buys tomorrow.

Shopping

Shopping in Milan can be very enjoyable – providing you have a deep pocket. Most shopoholics head for the **Quadrilatero d'Oro** (see page 23), where all the main fashion designers have their top stores. Those with shallower pockets could head for smaller stores in the Brera area or Corso Buenos Aires, Via Turino or the Navigli. Bargains are to be had with cast-off designer stock, end-of-season items and seconds. Remember, window shopping can be almost as gratifying as actually buying.

Milan has three **department stores** – the classy La Rinascente whose restaurant has a superb view of the pinnacles of the Duomo; Coin on the Piazza Cinque Giornate; and Upim in Piazza San Babila. **Retail hours** are normally 09:30–12:30 and 15:30–19:30. Some stores are closed Mon morning. During fashion fairs shops may stay open on Sun and Mon, while the lunch break tends to be disappearing. **Tax refunds**: non-EU citizens can reclaim value added tax (IVA) and there are refund centres at both of Milan's airports.

Shops

Giorgio Armani

Armani's store takes up a whole block and sells the latest designer wear plus perfumes, chocolates, flowers and alcohol. A restaurant and sushi bar provide sustenance.
⊠ *via Manzoni 31*
☎ *02 7231 8600*
M *Montenapoleone*

Gianni Versace

The kingpin of Milan's fashion, Versace was murdered outside his Florida home in 1997 and his funeral took place in Milan's Duomo. His luxuriant designs live on. There are two other stores apart from the main one.
⊠ *via Monte-napoloeone 11*
☎ *02 7600 8528*
M *San Babila*

La Perla

Lace and silk lingerie of the sexiest kind are the speciality of this sophisticated store.
⊠ *via Monte-napoleone 1*
☎ *02 7600 0460*
M *San Babila*

Les Amis

Famous women's shoe shop that can be relied on to sell something out of the ordinary. Specializes in boots.
⊠ *corso Garibaldi 127*
☎ *02 653 061*
M *Moscova*

Cut

Noted for high-quality artisan-made leather for men and women.
⊠ *corso di Porta Ticinese 58*
☎ *02 839 4135*
M *Porta Genova*

Libreria Internazionale Ulrico Hoepli

Founded in 1871, it sells books on any subject in any language, including English
⊠ *via Ulrico Hoepli 5*
☎ *02 864 871*
M *Duomo*

Controtempo

Marvellous selection of handbags, belts, jewellery and scarves.
⊠ *Corso di Porta Ticinese*
M *Duomo*

La Rinascente

This huge 8-floor department store has an indoor and outdoor rooftop café, an Estée Lauder spa and a hairdresser's.
⊠ *Piazza Duomo*
☎ *02 88 521*
M *Duomo*

Alessi

Probably the best-known name in Italian contemporary design, particularly when it comes to innovative homeware items.
⊠ *corso Matteotti 9*
☎ *02 795 726*
M *San Babila*

Market Sense

Sophisticated shoppers of the Quadrilatero d'Oro type would not be seen dead in Milan's many street markets, but as every experienced traveller knows, it is the marketplaces that give the real flavour of life in a country. Milan has a fascinating range of markets selling everything from junk through fashion bargains to quite sophisticated books and antiques. Some are covered, but most are found in the streets. Generally speaking the markets close at 13:00 and many close during the August holiday period. As with all crowded places, beware of pickpockets.

Markets
Fiera di Sinigaglia

This is Milan's top flea market, where you will be able to find a comprehensive range of junk, particularly ethnic goods.

⊠ *Viale Gabriele d'Annunzio, Darsena Naviglio*
⏱ *Sat 08:30–17:00*
M *Porta Genova*

Viale Papiniano

A wide-ranging flea market with clothing, shoes, homeware items, and there's always the chance of finding a designer bargain.

⊠ *Viale Papiniano West*
⏱ *Tue 08:30–13:00, Sat 08:30–17:00*
M *Sant'Agostino*

Mercatone dell' Antiquariato sul Naviglio Grande

Over 400 antique dealers sell items varying from snuff boxes to furniture in this narrow strip along the Naviglio Grande. Local restaurants stay open to cater for the visiting hordes.

⊠ *Strada Alzaia Naviglio Grande/Ripa di Porta Ticinese*
⏱ *last Sun of the month 09:00–17:00*
M *Porta Genova*

Mercato Comunale

Milan's main food market sells fruit, vegetables, fish, flowers, cheese and meat, much of it of high quality.

⊠ *Piazza Wagner*
⏱ *Mon 08:30–13:00,*

Right: *Souvenirs of Milan on sale, including ceramic plates showing the Duomo.*

*Tue–Sat 08:30–13:00
and 16:00–19:30*
M *Wagner*

Mercato di San Marco

This is another food market, with fruit, flowers and vegetables and a nice rowdy atmosphere.
⊠ *Via San Marco*
🕘 *Mon–Thu*
08:00–13:00
M *Moscova*

Mercato di Antiquari di Brera

Monthly antiques market with antique jewellery, textiles and furniture plus the possibility of an occasional bargain item.
⊠ *Via Fiori Chiari/Via Formentini*
🕘 *third Sun of the month 08:00–13:00*
M *Lanza*

Mercate Isola

Noted for its cut-price designer clothes and its ceramics from Tuscany.
⊠ *Piazzale Lagosta*
🕘 *Tue 08:30–13:00, Sat 08:30–17:00*
M *Garibaldi*

Fiera delli Oh Bei, Oh Bei

This unusual flea market is held in the square outside Sant'Ambrogio on the Saint's Day and named after the calls of the stallholders.
⊠ *Piazza Sant'Ambrogio*
🕘 *7 Dec annually 08:30–13:00*
M *Sant'Ambrogio*

Piazzetta Reale

A popular Sunday morning flower market.
⊠ *Piazzetta Reale*
🕘 *Mar–Jun and Sep–Dec, Sun 08:30–13:00*
M *Missori*

Above: *Picturesque canal-side flea market in the Navigli area.*

Fashionable Hats
The English word 'milliner' – a maker of hats, particularly for women – originates from Milan. The Milanese, from the 16th century onwards, have been Europe's foremost makers of hats, ribbons and gloves. Today, a wide range of hats can be bought in Milan, ranging from men's Panama straw hats to women's sophisticated fashion hats.

Above: *Milan has a wide variety of accommodation to suit all pockets and all tastes.*

Accommodation Tips
It is advisable to book accommodation well in advance, using fax, telephone or e-mail. A credit card number will usually be required in advance. When making a reservation, make sure that the price quoted includes IVA or sales tax, as this can add 10% to the cost. Most rates include breakfast, which will usually be a hot or cold buffet. At cheaper establishments it may be better to negotiate a room-only deal and slip out to a local café for breakfast.

WHERE TO STAY

Unlike many of the other Italian cities that provide accommodation largely for tourists, Milan tends to cater mainly for business travellers on a corporate budget. Accommodation is consequently expensive, particularly at the times when the trade fairs and fashion shows are taking place. During such times prices may rocket. Bringing a car to Milan is also a problem as few hotels can offer parking spaces, although some have pricey arrangements with local garages. Hotels in the city centre can also suffer from traffic noise, so try to book a room facing an inner courtyard.

All Italian hotels are categorized from one to five stars, based on the facilities offered, rather than the location, attraction or service. One- and two-star hotels still occasionally use the terms *pensione* or *locanda*. These are often family-run establishments and might not be able to offer guests a private bathroom. Three- and four-star hotels provide more facilities, including *en suite* bathrooms. Milan's five-star hotels are among the most luxurious in the world and offer the business traveller every convenience, including fax machines, computers and conference facilities. Many are located close to the Fiera, where the trade fairs are held.

The Duomo and Central Area

• *LUXURY*

Four Seasons
(Map C–F3)
Generally reckoned to be the best hotel in town with prices and services to match. Set in a converted 15th-century monastery with a delightful cloistered courtyard. Handy for the fashion district and some of the city's best restaurants.
⌧ *Via Gesu 8*, ☎ *02 77088*, ✆ *02 77985*, 💻 *www. four seasons.com/milan*
Ⓜ *Montenapoleone*

Grand Hotel et de Milan (Map C–E/F3)
Historic hotel located in a 19th-century palazzo, with Art Deco public rooms and antiques in the bedrooms. Suites named after famous guests like Verdi and Callas. Good restaurant.
⌧ *Via Manzoni 29*, ☎ *02 723 141*, ✆ *02 864 6861*, 💻 *www. granhoteletdemilan.it*
Ⓜ *Montenapoleone*

Grand Hotel Duomo (Map C–E4)
Many of the rooms overlook the spires of the Duomo. There is a newly refurbished wing with film and art themes. The hotel also has a spectacular roof terrace.
⌧ *Piazza del Duomo*, ☎ *02 8833*, ✆ *02 864620*, 💻 *www. grandhotelduomo.com*
Ⓜ *Duomo*

Spadari al Duomo
(Map C–E4)
This is a small individual hotel in one of the streets in the fashion quarter near the Duomo. It is full of artistic works by well-known Italians. Large rooms, many with jacuzzis.
⌧ *Via Spadari 11*, ☎ *02 723 141*, ✆ *02 861 184*, 💻 *www. spadarihotel.com*
Ⓜ *Duomo*

De la Ville
(Map C–E4)
An elegant hotel located between the Duomo and La Scala. It has well-furnished rooms, and there is a gym, Turkish baths and a conference centre. The quality and excellent service warrants the price.
⌧ *Via Hoepli 6*, ☎ *02 879 1311*, ✆ *02 866 609*, 💻 *www. delavillemilano.com*
Ⓜ *Duomo*

The Gray (Map C–F4)
Grey this is definitely not! The design is ultramodern and the minimalist rooms boast plasma screens and jacuzzis.
⌧ *Via San Raffaele 6*, ☎ *02 720 8951*, ✆ *02 866 526*, 💻 *www. hotelthegray.com*
Ⓜ *Duomo*

• *MID-RANGE*

Gran Duca di York
(Map C–F4)
Close to the cathedral, this former palazzo was once used to house visiting cardinals. Comfortable rooms, many with terraces.
⌧ *Via Montea 1a*, ☎ *02 874 863*, ✆ *02 869 0344*,
Ⓜ *Duomo*

Manzoni (Map C–F2)
Three-star hotel in the centre of the fashion district. There is a surcharge for breakfast and parking.
✉ *Via Santo Spirito 20,* ☎ *02 7600 5700,* 📠 *02 784 212,* 🖥 *www. hotelmanzoni.com*
Ⓜ *Montenapoleone*

• *BUDGET*
Gritti (Map C–E4)
A small modern hotel close to the Piazza Duomo. The noise from trams makes it essential to have an inward-facing courtyard room.
✉ *Piazza Santa Maria Beltrade 4,* ☎ *02 801 056,* 📠 *02 8901 0999,*
Ⓜ *Montenapoleone*

The North

This includes the area around the Stazione Central, the Castello Sforzesco and the Brera quarter.

• *LUXURY*
UNA Hotel Century (Map B–B3)
This is a modern tower block near the Central Station. It is designed to attract business customers with fax machines and computer points in each room. Attractive courtyard garden.
✉ *Via F. Filzi 25b,* ☎ *02 675 041,* 📠 *02 6698 0602,* 🖥 *www. unahotels.it*
Ⓜ *Centrale FS*

Excelsior Hotel Gallia (Map B–B3)
Close to the Stazione Centrale, this thirties-style establishment has every convenience for the business traveller with conference rooms and PC connections.
✉ *Piazza Duca d'Aosta 9,* ☎ *02 67851,* 📠 *02 6671 3239,* 🖥 *www.lemeridien-excelsiorgallia.com*
Ⓜ *Centrale*

• *MID-RANGE*
Antica Locanda Solferino (Map C–E1)
A small hotel located in the Brera district with only 11 rooms, all of which are furnished with antiques and original paintings. A homely touch is that your breakfast is served in your room with a newspaper.
✉ *Via Castelfidardo 2,* ☎ *02 657 0129,* 📠 *02 657 1361,* 🖥 *www.anticalocanda solferino.it*
Ⓜ *Moscova*

Marconi (Map B–B3)
Medium-sized hotel close to the Stazione Central. It has a pretty courtyard with lemon trees. There is a small conference room.
✉ *Via F. Filzi 3,* ☎ *02 6698 5561,* 📠 *02 669 0738,* 🖥 *www. marconihotel.it*
Ⓜ *Centrale*

Madisson (Map B–B3)
This is a friendly hotel located in a quiet side street just a short walk from the Stazione Centrale. Bed and breakfast only.
✉ *Via Gasparotto 8,* ☎ *02 6707 4150,* 📠 *02 6707 5059,*
Ⓜ *Centrale*

• *BUDGET*
London (Map C–D3)
Close to the Castello and a short walk to the Duomo. Some of

the rooms are small, but there is a 10% discount if the bill is paid in cash.
⊠ *Via Rovello 3,*
☎ *02 7202 0166,*
📠 *02 805 7037,*
💻 *www.hotel-london-milan.com*
M *Cairoli*

Ostello Piero Rotta
(Map B–A3)
This is Milan's only Youth Hostel. A large modern building in the suburbs near San Siro stadium. There is a 00.30 curfew! It is not possible to reserve ahead, so arrive early as it fills up quickly.
⊠ *Viale Salmoiraghi,*
☎ *02 3926 7095,*
🕐 *07:00–09:00 and 15:30–23:00,*
M *Lotto*

The East
• *LUXURY*
Sheraton Diana Majestic (Map C–H2)
Close to the Giardini Pubblici and the shops of the Corso Buenos Aires, this Liberty-style hotel was built on the site of a 19th century swimming pool.

Excellent amenities, elegant rooms and a shady courtyard.
⊠ *Viale Piave 42,*
☎ *02 20581,*
📠 *02 2058 2058,*
💻 *www.sheraton.com/dianamajestic*
M *PortaVenezia*

MID-RANGE
Mazzini (Map C–G1)
Located just southwest of the Giardini Pubblici, this family-run hotel is excellent value for money.
⊠ *Via Vitruvio 29,* ☎ *02 2952 6600,* 📠 *02 2951 0253,* 💻 *www.hotelmazzini.com*
M *Centrale*

• BUDGET
Aspromonte (Map B–C3)
Located on the square of the same name, the Aspromonte has basic amenities, but is good value for money. There is an attractive courtyard garden.
⊠ *Piazza Aspromonte 12/14,* ☎ *02 236 1119,* 📠 *02 236 7621,* 💻 *www.venere.it/milano/aspromonte*
M *Loreto*

Booking Accommodation
Many visitors to Milan will have booked their accommodation in advance through the internet, telephone or fax. There are travel agencies at Milan's two international airports who will book a hotel for you, but the choice will be limited to those hotels that pay a commission to the agencies. The **APT** office just off the Piazza Duomo will also book accommodation for a small fee (☎ 02 7252 4301, 💻 www.milanoinfotourist.com). They produce a comprehensive accommodation guide to Milan and the provinces that is updated every six months. Other useful contacts: **Hotel Reservation Center**, ⊠ Corso Buenos Aires 64, ☎ 02 2040 4099 **Centro Prenotazioni Hotel Italia**, ☎ 02 2940

Fiera di Milano
Trade fairs have been held in Milan since 1920. In the early years it was a temporary affair on the parade ground of the Castello Sforzesca, but in 1985 a permanent exhibition centre was set up. Today, it hosts over 70 specialist shows a year, attracting 5 million visitors and 10,000 firms. New hotels have clustered around the Fiera, but during trade-fair weeks, most of the decent hotels in the city will be full.

Sorting Out Your Trains
The Italian State Railways (*Ferrovie dellos Stato*) provide an excellent service with fares at bargains rates. There are many types of train and their varying speeds will affect journey times. *EuroCity* are international express trains, while *InterCity* trains provide a luxury service between Italian cities. *Expressos* are long-distance trains, which, despite their name, can be slow because they stop at many stations. The slowest trains are the *diretto* and the *locale*.

Kennedy (Map C–G1)
The best of numerous *pensione* in the Corso Buenos Aires/Giardini Pubblici area. Clean and friendly.
⊠ Viale Tunisia 6,
☎ 02 2940 0934,
M Republica

The South
• *LUXURY*
Liberty (Map C–F6)
Just to the east of the Navigli district, the Liberty has Art Nouveau décor and some rooms have jacuzzis. There is also an attractive court-yard garden.
⊠ Viale Bligny 56,
☎ 02 5831 8562,
✆ 02 5831 9061,
🖥 www.hotelliberty-milano.it

Carrobbio
(Map C–D5)
A small luxury hotel in an old back street to the southwest of the Duomo. Recently refurbished, with attractive rooms.
⊠ Via Medici 3,
☎ 02 8901 0740,
✆ 02 805 3334,
M Missori

• *MID-RANGE*
Regina (Map C–C5)
Housed in a con-verted 18th-century residence near the Navagli canals, the Regina has a comfort-able feeling about it. It is closed for the month of August.
⊠ Via Cesare Correnti 13, ☎ 02 5810 6913,
✆ 02 5810 7033.

Zurrigo (Map C–E5)
The Zurrigo is an eco hotel, protecting the environment by serving organic food and providing bicycles for its guests. It is situated within easy reach of the Duomo.
⊠ Corsa Italia 11,
☎ 02 7202 2260,
✆ 02 7200 0013,
M Missori

Ariston (Map C–D5)
Conveniently located between the Duomo and the Navigli dis-trict, the Ariston is another 'ecological hotel'; there are water saving devices, organic food is served and the lighting is energy efficient.

✉ *Largo Carrobbio 2,*
☎ *02 7200 0556,*
✆ *02 7200 0914,*
🖥 *www. brera
hotels.com/ariston*

Ca'Bianca

(Map C–B6)
A boutique hotel in
an old house on the
Naviglio Grande.
Some of the rooms
have balconies.
✉ *Via Lodovico il
Moro 117,*
☎ *02 8912 8111,*
✆ *02 8912 8042.*

The West

• LUXURY

Marriot (Map C–A4)
This is the ultimate
business hotel.
Located close to the
Fiera, the Marriot
boasts a whole floor
consisting of execu-
tive rooms, a well-
equipped business
centre, numerous
meeting rooms and
all the gadgetry the
corporate worker
could wish for.
✉ *Via Washington
66,* ☎ *02 4800 8981,*
✆ *02 4818 925,*
🖥 *www.mariott
hotels.com*

**Antares Hotel
Rubens** (Map C–A4)
Another business
hotel conveniently
close to the Fiera. The
top floor restaurant
has good views across
the city.
✉ *Via Rubens 21,*
☎ *02 40302,* ✆ *02
4819 3114,* 🖥 *www.
antareshotels.com*
M *De Angeli*

**Grand Hotel Fiera-
milano** (Map C–A1)
Located right outside
the Fiera. It has
modern rooms and all
the conference and
technology features
are available.
✉ *Viale S. Boezio 20,*
☎ *02 336 221,* ✆ *02
314 119,* 🖥 *www.
atahotels.com*
M *Amendola Fiera*

• MID-RANGE

**Antica Locanda
Leonardo** (Map C–B3)
A small, family-owned
hotel close to Santa
Maria del Grazie.
Once a 19th-century
palazzo, it has been
fully refurbished
recently in a tasteful
way with antiques

and fabrics. It has a
delightful courtyard,
positively dripping
with flowers.
✉ *Corso Magenta 78,*
☎ *02 463 317,*
✆ *02 4801 9012,*
🖥 *www.leoloc.com*
M *Cadorna*

Ariosto (Map C–B3)
This establishment is
situated in a classy
residential street
within easy reach of
both the Duomo and
the Fiera. The Ariosto
is noted for its Art
Nouveau staircase
and its attractive
patio garden.
✉ *Via Ariosto 22,*
☎ *02 481 7844,* ✆ *02
498 0516,* 🖥 *www.
hotelariosto.com*
M *Conciliazione*

• BUDGET

Vecchia Milano
(Map C–D4)
This small *pensione* is
located in a quiet
street to the west of
the Duomo. Will
appeal to families.
✉ *Via Borromei 4,*
☎ *02 875 042,*
✆ *02 8645 4292,*
M *Duomo*

Above: *Pasta comes in a vast variety of forms, often with imaginative sauces.*

EATING OUT
Food and Drink

Although few people would actually choose a holiday in northern Italy because of its food, one of the joys of visiting the area is to sample its cuisine and its wines. To be precise there is no such thing as typically Italian food, because there are a vast number of regional variations. Another popular misconception is that Italian food is all pasta and pizza. These do, of course, figure prominently on menus, but there are also some fine regional fish and meat dishes.

Food

Although many of Milan's hotels provide an international-style **breakfast**, the average Milanese does not make a big thing about this meal – breakfast is much more likely to be a quick coffee and a *brioche* taken standing at a bar.

Lunch, however, is a different matter. Many workers will take a long lunch with four courses (although others will prefer to have a light lunch and save the big meal for the evening). The meal starts with *antipasti* (literally 'before the pasta'). Similar to the French hors d'oeuvres, *antipasti* may be served buffet-style on a long table, often placed near the door of the restaurant to tempt diners in. Here a variety of items are on offer, including seafood, hams, mushrooms and salad from which you can make up your own assortment, known as *antipasto mista*.

A Variety of Pasta

A pasta course is an essential part of an Italian meal, but the pasta itself and the sauces that go with it vary tremendously. There are many varieties of pasta, depending on its shape. It can, for example, be tubular, flat, straw-like, twirled, conch-like, rolled or filled. It can also vary in its ingredients, with flour, eggs, oil and salt forming the basics. The sauces that are used to accompany the pasta change according to the region.

FOOD AND DRINK

The second course is known, confusingly, as the *primo piatto*. A soup is always on offer and this will either be a thick country soup or else a thin minestrone on which Parmesan cheese can be sprinkled. As the Lombardy Plain is a rice-growing area, a risotto is an alternative choice. These are often coloured yellow with saffron and may come with vegetables, meat or seafood. The third choice will involve pasta. There are said to be over 350 pasta shapes, but the most common are spaghetti, tagliatelle, lasagna, the meat-stuffed ravioli, and cannelloni. There are almost as many sauces to accompany the pasta, while Parmesan cheese is usually offered as a topping. Don't expect the waiter to come around with an enormous pepper grinder – this only happens in Italian restaurants abroad!

The main course is the *secondo piatto* and will be a fish or meat dish accompanied by a modicum of potatoes and vegetables. Regional specialities include *Cotoletta alla Milanese*, which is a veal slice dipped in egg and fried in breadcrumbs. Chicken (*pollo*), pork (*maiale*), beef (*manzo*) and lamb (*agnello*) are other meat choices. Another local speciality for those with strong stomachs is busecca, which is tripe with white beans. Fish is likely to be of the freshwater variety from the lakes to the north, and could include carp, trout or perch. Among the seafood, sea bass (*spigola*), red mullet (*triglia*) and swordfish (*pesce spada*) are often on the menu.

To complete the meal there will **cheese**, **desserts** or **fresh fruit**. Apart from the well-known blue-veined *gorgonzola* and *bel paese*, there is a whole host of local cheeses

Regional Differences in Cooking

The social and economic differences between the north and south of Italy are very noticeable. The comparison extends to cooking. Pasta in the north of Italy tends to be the flat variety, freshly made with eggs, whereas in the south the tubular varieties of pasta are more usual. In the north, the fat used for cooking is generally butter, while in the south olive oil is more popular. Flavours, particularly in sauces, are much stronger in the south, where full use is made of the Mediterranean aromatic herbs such as rosemary and thyme.

Italian or Austrian?

A local speciality of Milan is *Cotoletta* (or *costoletta*) *alla Milanese*. This is a slice of veal dipped in butter, coated in bread crumbs and then fried. Many people will recognize this as the Austrian *Wiener Schnitzel* and would automatically assume that this was a food relic of the 18th-century occupation. It may be the other way round, however, as it is claimed that one of the governors tasted it for the first time in Milan and brought the recipe back to Austria.

Tea and Coffee
The Italians are very enthusiastic coffee drinkers, and it comes in a bewildering variety. It is always made in an espresso machine – instant coffee is rarely an option. The choice is usually between a small black *espresso* or a larger white *cappuccino* (don't expect a topping of chocolate sprinkles). Other possibilities are a taller, weaker coffee (*Americano*), a tall coffee with a dash of milk (*macchiato*), and a tall milky coffee (*latte*). Many Italians like a drop of spirit in their drink – this is called *caffè corretto*. A popular choice in summer is to take coffee cold (*caffè freddo*). If it is topped with crushed ice and cream, you have *caffè granita*. Tea (*tè*) is much simpler. It comes either with lemon (*con limone*) or milk (*con latte*), but in summer cold tea (*tè freddo*) is also popular.

from all over the country. Italian desserts can be a delight or a disappointment, but you can't go wrong with Italian ice cream, particularly in Milan, which considers itself a specialist ice cream making area.

Visitors preferring a pizza should head for one of the specialist **pizzerias**, where the food is cooked in a traditional oven. The pizzas are usually thin and cooked to age-old recipes – don't expect any exotic toppings such as sweet corn or pineapple.

Drinks

Italy produces more **wine** than any other country in the world and much of it is from the Lombardy area. Probably the best-known wines are the light red (*rossi*) Valpollicellas and Bardolinos and the crisp white (*bianco*) Soaves grown to the east and south of Lake Garda. From the west of Lake Maggiore come the good quality red wines that include the full-bodied Barolo and the fragrant Barbaresco. Much of the wine exported from northern Italy in the past has been of only moderate standard but in more recent years higher quality wines have been produced. It is a good idea to try local wines – ask for *vino locale* or *vino della casa*. The Italians are certainly not wine snobs and frequently keep their lighter red wines in the fridge during the summer. Often their stronger white wines are not chilled at all.

Fortified wines include the usual *cinzano*, *martini* and *campari*. A wide variety of **spirits** are on sale. A popular local fire-water is *grappa*, which is drunk for effect rather than taste. Good local brandies include *stock* and *Vecchia Romagna*.

Opposite: *Among the many Italian spirits is the somewhat daunting grappa.*

Widely drunk **liqueurs** include *strega* (often taken with ice), the apricot-flavoured *amaretto*, cherry *maraschino* and the aniseed-tasting *sambuca*.

Beer (*birra*) comes in bottles or draught and is of the lager type. A small bottle is a *pícola* and a larger bottle is known as a *media*. There are also some darker beers available. Known as *birra nera*, they are sweeter and heavier and resemble English bitter. The local beers include Peroni, Moretti and Dreher, which are all excellent. If you don't ask for them you will probably be given foreign imported beers, which will be more expensive.

There are plenty of **soft drinks** to choose from, including a wide variety of fruit juices. Fizzy drinks include the ubiquitous cola and thirst-quenching lemon soda. Tap water is usually drinkable, but the Italians themselves drink vast amounts of bottled mineral water (*aqua minerale*), which comes either sparkling (*con gas*) or still (*naturale*).

Home-grown Firewater

Those wishing to have a drink for effect rather than for taste will find that **grappa** fits the bill. This colourless spirit gains its name from *graspa*, the detritus of the grapes after wine has been fermented. These dregs are then distilled to make grappa. It is produced in **Bassano di Grappa**, halfway between Lake Garda and Venice, but is available all over northern Italy. Its acquired taste being such, it is probably not surprising that it was used as a medicine in the Middle Ages!

The *Aperitivo* Scene

An alternative to a heavy (and probably expensive) dinner in Milan is to go to an *aperitivo* bar where snacks are served with drinks. The *aperitivo* scene starts around 18:00 and finishes as late as 21:00. The idea is to buy a round of drinks such as cocktails, sparkling or fortified wines and then help your self to snacks provided by the bar, much in the way of the Spanish tapas. Many of the bars now use the American term 'Happy Hour', although it lasts longer than one hour and there is rarely any reduction in the price of the drinks.

Yellow Risotto
Another speciality of Milan is *risotto alla Milanese* or, as it is sometimes known, *risotto con lo zafferano*. This is rice cooked slowly in stock with mushrooms and onions. It gets its name from a man called Zafferano who decided, as a gift to his wife on their wedding day, to colour his risotto yellow by adding saffron.

Below: *Italian restaurants use a variety of methods to attract diners.*

Where to Eat

Milan offers just about any food you can think about, such as local cuisine, food from other regions of Italy, bland international dishes and food from other countries including Chinese, Indian, Japanese and South American. One thing is certain: it will be more expensive than anywhere else in Italy, but still reasonable by London or New York standards.

Milan

• *LUXURY*
Savini

This establishment has been serving classic Milanese delicacies since 1867; it remains one of the top restaurants in the city.

✉ *Galleria Vittorio Emanuele II*
☎ *02 7200 3433*
🕓 *closed Sat evening and Sun*
M *Duomo*

La Scaletta

Fresh ingredients are used in creative recipes. This is one of the best restaurants in Milan.

✉ *piazza Stazione Porta Genova 3*
☎ *02 5810 0290*
🕓 *closed Sun and Mon lunchtime*
M *Porta Genova*

Aimo e Nadia

Family restaurant; consistently high standards. Many diners claim this to be the best in town.

✉ *via Montecuccoli 6*
☎ *02 416 886*
🕓 *closed Sun, Mon lunchtime, Aug*

Restaurants

Cracco-Peck

Elegant surroundings and creative food under the direction of Carlo Cracco earned this restaurant two Michelin stars. Classic Milanese dishes with a modern touch.
✉ via Victor Hugo 4
☎ 02 876 774 (reservations essential)
🕐 closed Sat, lunchtimes on Sun, and Aug
M Duomo

Il Teatro del Four Seasons

Located in the basement of a former convent now occupied by Milan's newest and best hotel. Mediterranean dishes and outstanding seafood.
✉ via del Gesu 8
☎ 02 7012 3476
🕐 closed Sat lunchtimes, Sun and Aug
M Montenapoleone

Boeucc

Founded in 1696 and based in an old palazzo, Boeucc is the altar of traditional Milanese cuisine. Formal clothes required.
✉ piazza Belgioioso 2

☎ 02 7602 2880
🕐 closed all day Sat, Sun lunchtime

Suntory Italia

Sophisticated atmosphere at what is the best Japanese restaurant in Milan.
✉ via Verdi 6
☎ 02 862 210
🕐 closed Sun
M Montenapoleone

Joia

Imaginative vegetarian restaurant near the Giardini Pubblici. Talented Swiss chef.
✉ via Castaldi 18
☎ 02 2952 2124 – booking advised
🕐 closed Aug
M Porta Venezia or Repubblica

• MID-RANGE
Trattoria Toscana Il Cerchio

This popular and homely trattoria is situated close to the Stazione Centrale.
✉ via Galvani 15
☎ 02 670 0738

Ponte Rosso

Excellent food is served in this friendly

Northern Specialities

Two northern products that are known worldwide are **prosciutto ham** and **Parmesan cheese**, which both come from the Parma area to the southeast of Milan. Parmesan cheese is left for two years to dry and mature and becomes stronger with age. Whey from the cheese is fed to the local pigs. Ham is carefully dried and salted to produce the delicately flavoured prosciutto. The region's products clearly bring profit – it is claimed that Parma has the highest standard of living of any city in Italy!

A Slice of Lemon

Putting a slice of lemon into an apéritif is a well-established habit in Milan. Lemons were once grown widely to the north of Milan, particularly in the Lakes region where they were introduced by monks in the 13th century. The town of Limone probably gets its name from the lemons cultivated on terraces along Lake Garda. Lemon growing is in decline, however, in Northern Italy. Milan now gets its lemons from the south of the country where they can be produced more cheaply without the danger of frost damage.

family establishment located alongside the Naviglio Grande.

✉ *ripa di Porta Ticinese 23*

☎ *02 837 3132*

I Malavoglia

Good Sicilian food, friendly atmosphere.

✉ *via Lecco 4*

☎ *02 2953 1387*

🕓 *closed Mon*

Trattoria Milanese

Run by the same family for nearly 100 years, this is one of the few trattorias in the city centre. Small restaurant, traditional food. Booking essential.

✉ *via Santa Marta 11*

☎ *02 8645 1991*

🕓 *closed Tue, Aug*

Ⓜ *Duomo*

Bistrot Duomo

Located on the top floor of La Rinascente department store, stunning views of the spires of the Duomo. Contempory food.

✉ *via San Raffaele 2*

☎ *02 877 120*

🕓 *closed lunch Sun, Mon and Aug*

Ⓜ *Duomo*

La Latteria

A small trattoria located in a former dairy. Lovingly prepared food attracting the fashion crowd.

✉ *via San Marco 24*

☎ *02 659 7653*

🕓 *closed Sat, Sun, Aug and Dec*

Ⓜ *Moscova*

Marino alla Scala

On the first floor of an old palace on Piazza della Scala. Modern décor and superb seafood. Cheaper café on the ground floor.

✉ *piazza della Scala 5*

☎ *02 8068 8201*

🕓 *closed Sun, Aug and Christmas*

La Libera

Traditional regional dishes, attracting the media crowd.

✉ *via Palermo 21*

☎ *02 805 3603*

Ⓜ *Moscova*

Officina 12

Waterfront Navigli restaurant. Jazz music and wood oven pizzas.

✉ *Alzala Naviglio Grande 12*

☎ *02 894 2261*

🕐 *closed Mon,
Sat–Tue lunch*
M *Porta Genova*

Don Carlos

In the Grand Hotel et de Milan. Verdi had an apartment here and there is much opera memorabilia. Perhaps surprisingly there is a modern menu.

✉ *via Manzoni 12*
☎ *02 7231 4640*
🕐 *open for dinner, closed Sun*
M *Duomo*

• BUDGET

There are any number of American fast-food outlets in Milan, where it is possible to eat cheaply. Pizzerias are also inexpensive, while many trattorias can be equally suitable for the budget-conscious. *Tavola Calda* (hot tables), where meals are taken standing up at the counter, are also affordable options.

Viel

One of a small chain of gelateria specializing in fruit shakes, ice cream and sorbets. Ideal on a hot day.

✉ *corso Buenos Aires 15*
☎ *02 2951 6123*
M *Lima*

Caffé della Pusteria

Good for a quick sandwich, pasta or a beer. Nice vine-covered terrace

✉ *via Edmundo de Amicis 22*
M *Sant'Ambrogio*

Camparino

A small café in the Galleria Victor Emanuele. The bar was once owned by the parents of David Campari, inventor of the famous drink.

✉ *Plaza del Duomo*
M *Duomo*

Above: *A visit to an Italian market is a highly recommended holiday experience.*

Wine Facts

Wine has been grown in Italy for more than 3000 years, so we need not be surprised that Italians are the greatest wine drinkers in the world, consuming 82 litres (143 pints) per capita per year. Italy also produces more wine than any other country – a massive 77 million hectolitres (1,700,000,000 gallons) annually, comprising a quarter of world production. Italy is also the only country in world where vines can be grown in every region in the land.

Pasterito/Pizzarito

Despite being in the centre of the city this is a bargain place for a cheap pizza or pasta.
✉ *via Verdi 6*
☎ *02 862 2100*
M *Duomo or Cordusio*

Warsa

Here's a surprise – an Eritrean restaurant. Cheap meat dishes, plus some vegetarian. Be prepared to eat with your fingers!
✉ *via Melso 16*
☎ *02 201 6730*
M *Porta Venezia*

Further Afield

• LUXURY
Ceresole

High-class Cremonese cuisine.
✉ *via Ceresole 4, Cremona*
☎ *0372 30990*

L'Aquila Nigra

All Mantua's local specialities in a frescoed dining room near the Palazzo Ducale.
✉ *via Vicolo Bonacolsi 4, Mantua*
☎ *0376 327 180*
🕐 *closed Mon*

Da Vittorio

One of Italy's top restaurants. Specializes in seafood.
✉ *via Giovanni XXIII 21, Bergamo*
☎ *035 218 060*
🕐 *closed Wed*

Hotel de la Ville's Derby Grill

Undoubtedly the best food in Monza.
✉ *viale Regina Margherita 15, Monza*
☎ *039 382 581*

Locanda Vecchia Pavia

Ancient restaurant serving local dishes in nouvelle cuisine style.
✉ *via Cardinal Riboldi 2, Pavia*
☎ *0382 304 132*

• MID-RANGE
Vesuvio

Reasonably priced local food.
✉ *piazza Libertà 10, Cremona*
☎ *0372 434 858*

Pavesi

Friendly restaurant, one of several in the atmospheric square. Local specialities.

✉ *Piazza dell'Erbe, Mantua*
☎ *0376 323 627*
🕐 *closed Thu*

Al Garibaldini

This restaurant is in a characterful house in Mantua's historic core.
✉ *via S. Longino 7, Mantua*
☎ *0376 328 263*
🕐 *closed Wed*

Due Cavallini

Located on the fringe of the historic centre of Mantua, this traditional trattoria gives value for money.
✉ *via Salmitro 5, Mantua*
☎ *0376 632 2084*
🕐 *closed Mon, Tue and mid-Jul to mid-Aug*

Taverna del Colleoni

Atmospheric restaurant in the old square; classical Italian food.
✉ *Piazza Vecchia, Bergamo*
☎ *035 232 596*
🕐 *closed Mon*

Antica Trattoria la Colombina

Ancient trattoria in old Bergamo. Traditional

food, great views from the terrace.

✉ *Via Borgo Canale, Bergamo*

☎ *036 261 402*

🕐 *closed Mon, Tue, and most of July*

Antica Osteria del Vino Buono

Friendly *osteria* next to the upper funicular station.

✉ *Piazza Mercato delle Scarpe, Bergamo,*

☎ *035 247 993.*

🕐 *closed Mon*

Dell'Uva

Regional food in the centre of town.

✉ *piazza Carrobiolo 2, Monza*

☎ *039 323 825*

Antica Osteria del Previ

On the Ticino River. Noted for frogs' legs, snails and river fish.

✉ *via Milazzo 65, Pavia*

☎ *0382 26203*

• *BUDGET*
Fragoletta Antica Osteria

Little ambience, but great cooking.

✉ *piazza Arche 5, Mantua*

☎ *0376 323 300*

🕐 *closed Mon*

Pizzeria Cremonese

Pizzas plus assorted local dishes.

✉ *piazza Roma 39, Cremona*

La Colombina

Terrace restaurant, local specialities.

✉ *borgo Canale 12, Bergamo*

☎ *035 261 402*

🕐 *closed Mon*

Piedigrotto

Serves good traditional pizzas.

✉ *corso Libertà 15, Mantua*

☎ *0376 327 014*

🕐 *closed Wed*

To Tip or Not to Tip?

It is always important for travellers to know whether or not tipping is expected. In Italy, a tip is always appreciated, but don't pay up unless the service is good. In restaurants, check the bill to see if service is included. If not, it is usual to add between five and ten per cent. In cafés and bars, a small tip will usually be sufficient. Porters in airports and hotels generally expect a small tip. On excursions, coach drivers and guides are normally rewarded if they have given good service. In the days of the lire the offer of coins was an insult. Today, euro coins are acceptable.

Below: *An eatery in the Galleria Vittorio Emanuele II.*

Above: *Milan has a thriving and vibrant nightlife, with a good choice of nightclubs, discos and restaurants with live music.*

ENTERTAINMENT
Nightlife

For whatever reason you find yourself in Milan, if you are looking for a good night out then you have come to the right place. There are clubs to satisfy every need, every taste and every age. Most of the city's nightclubs are located in the Brera, Corso Como or Navigli areas and stay open until 03:00 or 04:00. Many venues will feature live jazz, pop or rock music. Remember that the whole point of going to a club in Milan is to look your best, and there is always the chance of seeing a celebrity or a sports star. Indeed, many of city's famous footballers actually own clubs.

In recent years many nightclubs have introduced a pay-as-you-leave system, your ticket recording drinks, food and cloakroom use. When you settle your bill you will find that the cost of drinks, even the soft variety, is exorbitant, which may explain why the Milanese tend to go easy on the alcohol.

For information on what is happening around the clubs of Milan, take a copy of *Hello Milano* from the tourist office. Many bars also stock little pocket guides reviewing the club life of the city.

Music
Opera

Milan has been one of the world centres for opera ever since La Scala opera house (*see* page 16) first opened in 1778. All the

---

What's in a Name?
How did Milan get its name? The obvious answer is that it derives from either the Celtic 'midland' or the Roman Mediolanum, meaning 'in the middle of the plain' – Milan lies in the middle of the Plain of Lombardy between the Alps and the Apennines. Some authorities, however, claim that the name comes from *scrofa semilanuta*, the half-woolly bear, which was the city's emblem in pre-Roman times.

famous conductors and opera singers have performed here over the years and many have lived in the city or studied at the music school. La Scala was closed during World War I and badly damaged during World War II. In the early years of the 21st century the opera house was closed for renovation, reopening in 2005.

A large proportion of the auditorium is given over to boxes, which indicates the status of the opera house in Milan society and the operatic knowledge of the city's inhabitants. They are not prepared to put up with what they consider poor performances, even if these are given by world famous singers. The Milanese also had strong opinions as to how La Scala should be renovated and there were noisy protests about plans to demolish the backstage area. Needless to say, tickets for a first night performance are both expensive and difficult to obtain.

All the World's a Stage

The stage at La Scala Opera House is one of the largest in the world, measuring 1200m² (13,000 sq ft). Beneath the stage is the orchestra pit. Until 1907 the orchestra had played on the same level as the stalls. The large stage also accommodates the theatre's corps de ballet, many of whose members come from La Scala's Ballet School.

Below: *La Scala, Milan's world-famous opera house, seen from the orchestra pit. It was built in 1776 on the site of the Church of Santa Maria della Scala.*

Auditorium di Milano
✉ largo Mahler 1
☎ 02 8338 9201
🖥 www.audtorium
dimilano.org

Conservatorio di Musica 'Giuseppe Verdi'
✉ via Conservatorio 12
☎ 02 762 1101
🖥 www.conservatorio-milano.com

Teatro Dal Verme
✉ via San Giovanni sul Muro 2
☎ 02 8700 5201
🖥 www.dalverme.org

Classical Music

There are a number of venues for more serious music in Milan. The most prominent is the **Auditorium di Milano**. This is the home of the city's Verdi Orchestra and choir. Seating nearly 1500 people, the auditorium's acoustics are highly rated. Rather cheaper is the **Conservatorio di Musica 'Giuseppe Verdi'** where you can hear the students playing classical items. In addition there is the **Teatro Dal Verme**. Dating back to 1872, the theatre became a cinema after World War II, but was closed for over 20 years before re-opening as a theatre in 2001. Its classical music programme features a number of visiting orchestras.

Opposite: *The Ariosto is one of Milan's 113 cinemas.*
Below: *Ornate wrought iron work embellishes the Conservatoire di Musica 'Giuseppe Verdi'.*

Jazz, Rock and Pop

Milan is the centre of Italy's music industry. Spurred by the importance of La Scala, the city has long produced sheet music. Now it has a number of recording studios and as a result many artists have come to live in Milan, which in turn has encouraged a

good degree of home grown talent. Venues vary from the mega spots – **Filaforum**, **Mazda Palace** and **Stadio Meazza** (San Siro) to small intimate clubs and cafés where entrance may be free. Jazz is becoming increasingly popular in Milan and a number of jazz cafés and restaurants have sprung up, mainly in the Navgli area, such as **Scimmie** (see page 77), which also incorporates a canal boat. The Blue Note, a follow-up of the original Blue Note in

New York's Greenwich Village, opened in 2001 and has already proved a great success, attracting some notable musicians.

Theatre

Live theatre has always been the poor relation of opera in Italy. One of the problems has been that on the unification of Italy there were a number of regional languages and dialects and no natural theatre prose language. In Milan there are over 30 small theatres – usually with fewer than 500 seats – based in halls and churches, with plays usually acted out in the Milanese dialect. Not surprisingly, plays are rarely advertised for tourists.

Cinema

Film, on the other hand, has increased in popularity, and many theatres have been converted into cinemas. Foreign films are usually dubbed, although with Milan's increasing immigrant population, a number of films are being shown in the original language. Film showings are usually continuous from early afternoon till midnight. Some of the better cinemas are **Ariosto**, **Cinema Mexico** and **Odeon**. There is also a **Museo del Cinema** (see page 38).

Milan hosts two annual film festivals, the **Film Festival Internazionale di Milano**, which is held in early November, and the **Milano Film Festival** which takes place in mid-September.

Filaforum
✉ via D. Vittorio 6
☎ 199 128 800
🖥 www.forumnet.it

Mazda Palace
✉ via Sant'Elia 33
☎ 02 3340 0551
🖥 www.mazdapalace.it

Stadio Meazza (San Siro)
✉ viale Piccolomini 5
☎ 02 4870 7123

Blue Note
✉ via Borsieri 37
☎ 02 6901 6888
🖥 www.bluenote
milano.com

Ariosto
✉ via L. Ariosto 16

Cinema Mexico
✉ via Savona 57

Odeon
✉ via Santa Radegonda 8

Right: *Inter Milan versus Parma at San Siro stadium.*
Opposite: *Horse racing at the San Siro racecourse close to the stadium.*

Festival Calendar
• 6 Jan – **Epiphany**; procession of the Three Kings.
• Mid-Jan – **Milano Moda Uomo**; mens' fashion week, autumn and winter collections.
• Feb – **Carnevale Abrosiano**.
• Late Feb – **Milano Moda Donna**; main fashion week, women's autumn and winter fashions unveiled.
• Mar – **Sant' Ambrogio Carnival**.
• Mar – **BIT**; the international tourism trade fair at the Fiera.
• Mar, third weekend – **Giornata FAI di Primavera**; many historic monuments and palazzi open to the public.
• Mid-April – **Salone Internazionale del Mobile**; the international furniture fair at the Fiera.
• April, third Sun – **Mercato dei Fiori**; flower fair along the Navigio Grande.
• April – **Gitta di Milano**; jazz festival.
• May – **Milano Cortili Aperti**; secret courtyards open to public.
• May – **Pittori sul Navigio**; outdoor art festival along the banks of the Alzaia Naviglio.

Spectator Sports

Of the spectator sports, football (*calcio*) is almost like a religion. The Italian League is divided into four divisions, the most prestigious of which is called Serie A. Matches are played in winter, usually on Saturday afternoons at San Siro Stadium (*see page 33*).

Other popular spectator sports have been imported from America and include basketball and baseball. Also keenly followed is motor racing, and an annual Grand Prix is held at Monza just north of Milan. Cycling, too, is popular with both riders and spectators, and the weekend roads are full of recreational and competitive cyclists.

Gambling

Milanese looking for a flutter on the horses head for the **Ippodromo** next to San Siro soccer stadium. Meetings are held all year except for December. Evening races are held from June to September. While at the Ippodromo, be sure to take a look at *Il Cavallo*, a huge statue of a horse. It was made in America and erected in 1999 based on the designs of Leonardo da Vinci some 500 years earlier.

Festivals and Fairs

Milan's festivals and other cultural events show the city in two different lights. One shows the traditional and religious face, the other the commercial side of life in Milan. Some festivals remain purely religious, such as **Epiphany** on 6 January, when a procession of the Three Wise Men goes from the Duomo to the church of Sant' Eustorgio. The religious origins have been adapted to show a secular face in Milan's **Carnevale**, a carnival that takes place in the days following Shrove Tuesday. Carnivals in the rest of the world normally end on Mardi Gras, but Archbishop Ambrose decreed that the carnival should continue until the following Saturday, which was probably why they made him a saint! The Carnevale today has processions with floats and a fancy dress parade with much confetti throwing in the Piazza del Duomo.

The more commercial aspect of Milan's festivals is shown in its numerous **trade fairs**. The city's main **fashion week** takes place in late February, when scores of designers unveil their autumn and winter collections. The women's spring and summer fashions are displayed in October.

Festival Calendar

- May – **International Antiques Fair** at the Fiera.
- Jun – **Festa del Navigli**; street artists, concerts, antique markets and much more.
- Jun – **Milano d'Estate**; open-air concerts and other cultural events in the Parco Sempione and grounds of Castello Sforzesco.
- Jun, third Sun – **Sagra di San Cristoforo**; the patron saint of travellers is celebrated outside the tiny church of San Cristoforo; decorated boats sail on the canal.
- Jun – **Orticola**; flower show in the public gardens, Porta Venezia area.
- Jun – **Milano Moda Uomo**; men's fashion week, spring and summer collections.
- July – **Festival Latino Amercando**; Latin American music, food, dance and cinema.
- July – **Arianteo**; outdoor film festival.
- Aug – **Ferragusto**; feast of the Assumption.
- Sep – **Milano Film Festival**.
- Oct – **Milano Moda Donna**; fashion week, in which designers present their spring and summer collections.
- Oct – **SMAU**; International Multimedia show at the Fiera.
- Oct – **Fiera di Chiaraville**; fair at the Cistercian Abbey, with music, dancing and art exhibitions.

Above: *A disc jockey plies his trade at one of Milan's many clubs.*

Men, too, have their fashion trade fairs in June and October. The majority of firms use the Fiera for their catwalk displays, but a few of the major names now use other venues. Armani, for example, uses the old Nestlé factory, while Prada locates in a renovated warehouse.

Other industries have trade fairs too. There is a **tourism** fair in March, an **arts and crafts** fair in December, while the world-renowned **furniture** trade show takes place in mid-April. The **film industry** has two important festivals, one in September and the other in November. The most keenly attended is the **Milano Film Festival** held in the Piccolo Teatro at Castello Sforzesco. There are international competitions, workshops, open-air screenings and, of course, the associated parties.

The Navigli area provides a wonderful setting for a number of lower key fairs and festivals, with an **art** show in early May and an international **antiques** fair later in the month. The Navagli also has its own jamboree on the first Sunday of every month from June to September.

Festival Calendar
• Nov – **Internazionale di Milano Film Festival**.
• Nov – **Expo dei Sapori**; Italian regional food fair at the Fiera.
• Dec – **Festa di Sant' Ambrogio**, which includes the **Fiera degli** *Oh bej Oh bej* street fair.
• Dec – **L'Artigiano**; Milan crafts fair, held in the Fiera.

Nightclubs, Bars and Discos

Rolling Stone

Milan's most important rock venue, three floors. Music beats out as loudly as the group it was named after.

⊠ corso XII Marzo 32
☎ 02 733 172
🖳 www.rollingstone.it
🕐 11:00–04:00 Thu–Sun

Scimmie

Jazz bar featuring nightly live music; also a restaurant, pizzeria and canal barge.

⊠ Via Asciano Sforza
☎ 02 8940 2874
🖳 www.scimmie.it
🕐 19:00–05:00 daily

Casablanca Café

Moroccan themed disco bar and restaurant.

⊠ corso Como 14
☎ 02 6269 0186
🖳 www.casablanca cafe.it
🕐 18:30–15:00 Tue–Sun

B4

Popular disco and aperitivo bar, occasional art exhibitions.

⊠ via Ripamonti 13
☎ 02 5830 5632
🕐 18:00–02:00

Rocket

Entry to this disco and cocktail bar is free.

⊠ via Pezzotti 52
☎ 02 8950 3509
🖳 www.therocket.it
🕐 21:00–15:00

Tasca

Spanish-style tapas bar, popular with tourists and locals.

⊠ corso di Porta Ticinese 17
☎ 02 832 2899
🕐 Tue–Sun

El Brellin

Bar, restaurant and live music venue on Navigli waterfront.

⊠ Alzaia Navigli Grande 14
☎ 02 5810 1351
🕐 closed Sun

Torqueville 13

Good-quality nightclub and restaurant popular with footballers and models.

⊠ via Torqueville 13
☎ 02 2900 2973
🕐 22:00–05:00 daily, closed Jul, Aug

Gay and Lesbian Clubs

Perhaps because of the fashion and music industries, Milan's gay community are given a high level of acceptance. There are plenty of gay bars and clubs in the city.

G Lounge

A popular aperitivo haunt before attracting the gay crowd later in the evening.

⊠ via Larga 8
☎ 02 805 3042
🖳 www.glounge.it
🕐 07:00–02:00 Tue–Sat, 22:00–00:00 Sat; closed Aug

Nuovo Idea

Milan's first gay club, still going strong. Popular with transvestites.

⊠ via de Castillia 30
☎ 02 6900 7859
🕐 22:30–05:00

Plastic

Classy interior, avant-garde crowd; Sun is gay-friendly night.

⊠ viale Umbria 120
☎ 02 733 996
🕐 20:00–04:00, closed Aug

Above: *The dome of the Basilica of Santa Maria Maggiore – Bergamo's finest church.*

EXCURSIONS

Milan is a handy centre for visiting a number of ancient cities and abbeys on the Plain of Lombardy. In many cases these towns flourished during the Dark Ages or the Middle Ages, but since then they have been left behind by Milan's determined growth. Fortunately this has meant that the towns have retained their old cobbled streets, ancient buildings and medieval atmosphere. **Bergamo**, for example, has a superb Old Town set up on a hill and protected by fortifications. **Pavia**, to the south of Milan, has retained its old Roman street plan and has an imposing Visconti castle and an ancient university. **Cremona**, away to the east, has a magnificent cathedral. It was the birthplace of Monteverdi and is noted for its manufacture of violins. Surrounded by lakes and swamps, **Mantua** is famous for its atmospheric squares. It was ruled by the wealthy Gorzaga family for centuries and they encouraged artists such as Andreas Mantegna to base themselves here under their patronage.

You can leave Milan behind and within an hour be in the **Italian Lakes** region. Lakes such as Como, Maggiore and Garda are long and narrow in shape and owe their origins to the Ice Age, when glaciers moved down from the Alps, eroding deep valleys that later filled with meltwater. The shores are graced by elegant villas and tree-lined promenades backed by terraces of citrus fruit and olives, with the snowcapped Alps forming a stunning backdrop.

Condottieri

Condottieri were soldiers of fortune in the service of Italian states during the late Middle Ages. One of the most famous condottieri was **Bartolomeo Colleoni** (1400–76), a native of Bergamo who fought for and against most of the ruling dynasties of his time. The rebus of this fighting man says it all – it was in the form of *coglioni* (testicles) and appears on his coat of arms. The **Colleoni Chapel** at Bergamo, which he had built as a personal mausoleum, is one of the most stunning pieces of architecture in northern Italy – a fitting memorial for an old soldier.

Bergamo

Bergamo was an independent city-state or *comune* in the 12th century, but after 1329 it came under Visconti control. For the next 350 years it was an outpost of the Venetian Empire – which explains the large number of statues of Venetian lions around the city.

Bergamo is divided into two parts – the hilltop settlement of **Città Alta**, ringed by Venetian defensive walls, and **Città Bassa**, which spreads across the plains below.

In the modern **Città Bassa** we find the **Museo Donizettiano**, named after the locally born opera composer. There is an excellent art gallery, the **Pinacoteca dell'Accademia Carrara**. Housed in an old palace in Via San Tomaso, it has works by Botticelli, Bellini, Titian, Van Dyck and Brueghel.

In the **Città Alta** is the charming Piazza Vecchia, dominated by the 12th-century **Torre Civica**, some 52m (170ft) high. The belfry has a 15th-century clock, and a huge bell still tolls 180 times at 22:00 for the nightly curfew. At the upper end of the Piazza Vecchia is the 12th-century **Palazzo della Ragione**, which can only be visited when it is staging an exhibition.

The **Basilica of Santa Maria Maggiore** is one of the finest Romanesque churches in northern Italy. The interior is stunning, with superb Flemish tapestries. Donizetti's tomb is tucked away against the west wall. In the presbytery there are some wonderful examples of *tarsias* – inlaid woodwork – showing Old Testament scenes.

The 1470s **Colleoni Chapel** next door was designed by Amadeo for the tomb of the *condottiere* Bartolomeo Colleoni. Excellent paintings by Tiepolo line the dome.

Bergamo
Location: Map G
Distance from Milan:
51km (31 miles)

Museo Donizettiano
✉ via Arena 9
☎ 035 399 269
🕐 10:00–13:00 and 14:30–17:00 Tue–Sun Apr–Sep; 10:00–13:00 Tue–Sun Oct–Mar

Pinacoteca dell'Accademia Carrara
✉ piazza G Carrara 82a
☎ 035 399 640
🖥 www.accademia carrara.bergamo.it

Torre Civica
✉ Piazza Vecchia
☎ 035 247 116
🕐 09:30–19:00 Tue–Sun Apr–Oct; 09:30–16:30 Tue–Fri Nov–Mar

Palazzo della Ragione
✉ Piazza Vecchia
☎ 035 210 204
🕐 10:00–13:00 and 14:30–17:00 Tue–Sun Apr–Sep; 10:00–13:00 Tue–Sun Oct–Mar

Basilica of Santa Maria Maggiore
✉ Piazza del Duomo
☎ 035 223 327
🕐 Mon–Sat 09:00–13:00 and 15:00–18:00 year-round; Sun 14:30–16:30 Apr–Oct; Sun 09:00–12:00 and 14:30–16:30 Nov–Mar

Colleoni Chapel
✉ Piazza del Duomo
☎ 035 210 223
♿ admission free

Pavia

Pavia
Location: Map F
Distance from Milan
35km (22 miles)

**Basilica di San
Michele Maggiore**
✉ Piazza San Michele
☎ 0382 26 062
🕓 07:30–12:00 and
15:00–19:00 daily

Museo Civico
✉ Piazza Castello
☎ 0382 33 853
🕓 10:00–12:00 and
14:30–16:00 Tue–Sun

Certosa di Pavia
✉ via del
Monumento 5
☎ 0382 925 613
🕓 09:00–11:30 and
14:30–17:30 Tue–Sun;
closing times may vary
in summer and winter.

Dominating the core of the town is the rather stolid looking **Duomo**; its huge 19th-century dome, the third largest in Italy, towers above the rooftops. Far more attractive than the Duomo is the **Basilica di San Michele Maggiore**, a fine Romanesque church dating back to 661. It has some decorative sculpture, both on the frieze on the sandstone façade and on the capitals of the main columns in the interior. Also look for the Romanesque mosaic in the presbytery.

Castello Visconteo, built in 1360, was partially destroyed in the Battle of Pavia in 1525. Three sides survive and they now house the **Museo Civico**, which contains an excellent archaeological section. The art gallery has some important works by Italian and Dutch painters.

The River Ticino in Pavia is straddled by an attractive covered bridge, the **Ponte Coperto**. The original medieval covered bridge was just to the east, but was destroyed during World War II.

The **Certosa di Pavia** was built by Gian Galeazzo Visconti in the 1390s as a family mausoleum. The stunning façade was designed by Giovanni Antonio Amadeo. It became a Carthusian monastery, but this was suppressed by Napoleon. In 1968 a group of Cistercian monks took over the monastery and now conduct guided tours. For more information, see page 33.

Below: *The Ponte Coperto or Covered Bridge spans the River Ticino in Pavia.*

Cremona

Cremona's Piazza del Comune is dominated by the 112m (370ft) **Torrazzo**. Built around 1250, it is reputedly the tallest bell tower in Italy. There are 502 steps to the top, but the climb is rewarded with exceptional views. Next to the tower, linked to it by a portico, is the **Duomo**. Features of interest include the primitive frescoes, Flemish tapestries, the twin pulpits, and beautiful choir stalls inlaid with views of Cremona.

Also in the Piazza del Comune are the 1167 **Battistero di San Giovanni**, and the **Loggia dei Militi** with an outdoor pulpit used by popular preachers of the time. Behind the loggia is the 1206 **Palazzo del Comune**. It is now the town hall.

Cremona is famous for its violins. The industry was started in the 16th century by the Amati family and followed on by Guarneri and Stradivarius. Today more than 50 violin-makers keep up the tradition. A comprehensive view of the subject can be enjoyed at the **Museo Stradivariano**, with more memorabilia at the **Museo Civico**, which also has a good section on archaeology. The School of Violin and Viola Makers also has a museum of stringed instruments at the **Palazzo dell'Arte**.

Mantua (Mantova)

Mantua's **Palazzo Ducale** is huge; when it was ransacked in 1630, it is said that it took 80 carriages to take away the 2000 works of art. Visits are by guided tour only and take about 1½ hours. The highlights are the **Camera degli Sposi**, containing Mantegna's frescoes of the Gonzaga family, and the private **apartments of Isabella d'Este**.

Above: *Cremona's graceful Duomo was built by the Comacini masters in the 12th century.*

Cremona
Location: Map D–F5
Distance from Milan: 84km (52 miles)

Torrazzo
✉ Piazza del Comune
☎ 0372 27 633
🕐 10:00–13:30 Tue–Sun

Duomo
✉ Piazza del Comune
🕐 07:30–12:00 and 15:30–19:00 Mon–Sat, 07:30–13:00 and 15:30–19:00 Sun

Museo Stradivariano
✉ via Pedestro 17
🕐 08:30–18:00 Tue–Sat, 10:00–18:00 Sun, closed Aug

Museo Civico Ala Ponzone
✉ Palazzo Affaitati
☎ 0372 31 222
💻 www.comune.cremona.it
🕐 09:00–18:00 Tue–Sat, 10:00–18:00 Sun

Above: *Rotonda di San Lorenzo, oldest church in Mantua.*

Mantua
Location: Map H
Distance from Milan:
152km (94 miles)

Palazzo Ducale
✉ Piazza Sordello
☎ 0376 352 100
🕐 09:00–18:30
Tue–Sun

Rotonda di San Lorenzo
✉ Piazza Erbe
🕐 10:00–13:00 and
14:00–18:00 Mon–Fri,
10:00–18:00 Sat

Basilica di Sant'Andrea
✉ Piazza Mantegna
☎ 0376 328 504
🕐 07:30–12:00 and
15:00–19:00
🔓 admission free

Palazzo Tè
✉ Viale Tè
☎ 0376 323 266
🕐 13:00–18:00 Mon,
09:00–18:00 Tue–Sun

Opposite the Palazzo Ducale is the **Duomo**. It was built in the 13th century and shows a mixture of styles. On the other side of the square are the **Bonacolsi Palaces**, with the notorious **Torre della Gabbia**, said to contain an iron torture cage in which prisoners were suspended over the city.

Mantua's oldest church, the 11th-century **Rotonda di San Lorenzo**, is said to be modelled on the Church of the Holy Sepulchre in Jerusalem. It has been sympathetically restored and you can see some 12th- and 13th-century frescoes.

Nearby is the **Basilica di Sant'Andrea**. The crypt houses two sacred reliquaries said to contain the blood of Christ, given to St Andrew by Longinus, the Roman centurion who pierced Christ's side with a lance.

On the southern outskirts of Mantua is the **Palazzo Tè**. Designed by Giulio Romano, it is considered to be his greatest work. The main attraction is a series of rooms with extraordinary frescoes, *trompe l'oeil* and paintings, showing that Romano was given full permission to shock and amaze. Many of the classical frescoes are erotic, even vaguely pornographic, but never dull.

The Italian Lakes

The five large lakes, and many small ones, are deep and steep-sided; with the snowy backdrop of the Alps, they form Italy's most stunning scenic area. In winter they are milder than the Plain of Lombardy, allowing subtropical plants to flourish, while in summer a cool breeze from the Alps moderates the heat and provides ideal conditions for water sports such as sailing and windsurfing.

The nearest lake, under an hour's drive by motorway from Milan, is **Lake Como**. The ancient of city of Como, with its fine cathedral, lies at the southern end of the lake. Further north are pretty lakeside villages like Bellagio, Menaggio and Varenna.

Just to the west of Lake Como is the smaller and more remote **Lake Lugano**. Largely in Switzerland, it has as its largest town the elegant Lugano.

Further west is **Lake Maggiore**, probably the most fashionable of the lakes, with up-market resorts such as Stresa and Verbania. Off-shore lie the Borromean Islands, once the home of the the Borromeo family, rulers of this area in the 15th century. Maggiore is notable for its opulent villas with their colourful gardens.

Tiny **Lake Orta** is just 13km (8 miles) in length. Few can resist the charms of the lakeside village of Orta San Giulio and the hill behind it with some 21 chapels.

The most distant lake from Milan, some two hours' drive east from the city, is **Lake Garda**. The largest and most commercialized of the Italian Lakes, its two shores make for a marked contrast. The western shore is steep-sided with terraced citrus groves and a series of charming lakeside villages, such as Gardone, Limone and Riva. The eastern side is lower-lying and covered with vineyards producing some of Italy's finest wines. Here you will find **Gardaland** (see page 49), a theme park designed for family enjoyment.

Italy's Lakes

It is estimated that there are around 1500 lakes in Italy. They have been formed in various ways. The most common are **alpine glacial lakes**, which are small, usually round and occupy cirques where glaciers were originally formed. **Crater lakes** are found in the craters of extinct volcanoes, mainly in the south of Italy. **Coastal lakes** are in the form of lagoons and can be seen along the Adriatic coast. The largest and most scenically spectacular lakes are the **ribbon lakes**, such as Lake Como in northern Italy, which occupy the over-deepened valleys carved out by glaciers in the Ice Age.

Below: *Lake Maggiore, with the Borromean Islands, viewed from Stresa.*

Above: *The Milan metro is cheap, effective and the best way to get around the city.*

Fact File on Milan
Size: covers an area of 182km² (70 sq miles).
Position: 122m (400ft) above sea level in the Po Basin.
Population: 1.4 million. Milan is the second largest city in Italy and the 10th largest in Europe. Greater Milan has a population of 3.78 million.
Population density: 1900 per km² .
Education: Milan has three universities, as well as the country's most prestigious business school, a polytechnic, and academies of music and art.

Tourist Information

The **Italian State Tourist Office** (ENIT) has offices abroad in the USA (New York, Los Angeles and Chicago), Canada (Montreal and Toronto), Australia (Sydney) and the Republic of Ireland. The address of the UK office is: ⊠ 1 Princes St, London, W1R 8AY, ☎ 020 7408 1254, ℘ 020 7493 6695. These offices are useful before departure, providing brochures, maps, transport and accommodation details. Within Italy there are regional and provincial tourist boards. All cities, towns and airports will have a tourist office usually known as an **APT** (*Azienda per il Turismo*) and shown with the standard '**i**' symbol. APT's are found in the following towns and cities:

Milan: ⊠ via Marconi 1, (next to the cathedral), ☎ 02 7252 4301, ℘ 02 7252 5250. There is also an office at the Stazione Centrale, ☎ 02 669 0432, 🖥 www.vivamilano.it
Bergamo: ⊠ viale Vittorio Emanuele II 20, ☎ 035 213 185, ℘ 035 230 184, 🖥 www.bergamo.it
Brescia: ⊠ corso Zanadelli 38, ☎ 030 45052, ℘ 030 293 284, 🖥 www.bresciaholiday.com
Como: ⊠ piazza Cavour 17, ☎ 031 269 712, ℘ 031 261 152, 🖥 www.lakecomo.com
Cremona: ⊠ Piazza del Comune (opposite the cathedral), ☎ 0372 23233, 🖥 www.cremonaturismo.com
Monza: ⊠ Piazza Communale, ☎ 039 323 222.
Pavia: ⊠ via F. Filzi 2, ☎ 0382 22156, ℘ 32221.

Stresa: ✉ Via Principe Tomaso, ☎ 0323 30150, 📠 0323 32561, 🖥 www.lagomaggiore.it
Varese: ✉ via Carrobio 2, ☎ 0332 283 604.
Verona: ✉ Piazza Brà, ☎ 045 806 8680, 🖥 www.verona-apt.net

Entry Requirements

All visitors to Italy need a valid passport. Citizens of EU countries, including the UK and the Republic of Ireland, can stay as long as they like. Visitors from the USA, Australia, Canada and New Zealand can stay up to 3 months without a visa. Visitors from other countries should consult their embassies regarding visas. It is a legal necessity to register with the police within three days of entering Italy – your hotel or camp site automatically does this for you. Anyone on holiday who registers with the local police station will probably be greeted with baffled amusement!

Customs

EU regulations allow a free exchange of non-duty-free goods for personal use for citizens of these countries. There is little point in bringing in duty-paid goods as tobacco and alcohol are as cheap or cheaper here than in other European countries. Visitors from non-EU countries are subject to restrictions which vary from country to country. The age limit for importing alcohol and tobacco is 17. There is no limit on the amount of traveller's cheques that can be imported or exported.

Health Requirements

The standard of health care in northern Italy is generally on a par with the rest of Europe and travellers should encounter few problems. EU residents should take Form E111 with them so that they can obtain treatment on the same terms as residents. Australia also has a reciprocal health care agreement, but visitors from other countries should take out travel insurance that includes health benefits. For minor problems, go to the nearest *farmacia*, open normal shopping hours. There is generally a duty pharmacy open at other times. In Milan there is a 24-hour *farmacia* at the Stazione Centrale.

Getting There

By air: Milan has two airports, Linate and Malpensa. **Linate** (info ☎ freephone 1673 37337) is 8km (5 miles) east of the city centre. The two national airlines, British Airways (☎ 848 812 266) and Alitalia (☎ 848 865 641), run scheduled flights to Milan Malpensa. The city is also served by several budget airlines: **British Midland** (🖥 www.ifly-britishmidland.com), **Easyjet** (🖥 www.go-fly.com), **Ryanair** (🖥 www.ryanair.com) and **Sky Europe** (🖥 www.skyeurope.com). In the future Linate will only do domestic flights. **Malpensa** (☎ freephone 7485 2200) is 50km (31 miles) northwest of Milan. Terminal One handles international flights and Terminal Two does charters. Both **British Airways** (info ☎ 0345 222 111) and **Alitalia** (info ☎ 020 760 2711) offer daily flights to and from London. Alitalia also has connections with the USA. Main international car hire firms have offices at Malpensa, but many prefer to use public transport to Milan. A high-speed railway line connects airport and city, with trains at 30-minute intervals. There are two efficient coach lines. The Malpensa Shuttle drops you at Stazione Centrale, and the Malpensa Express connects with Stazione Centrale and Piazzale Cadorna. Both coach lines run at 20-minute intervals. Passengers visiting Lake Garda can use British Airways flights to **Verona**.

By road: The UK is linked with Europe by car ferry and the Channel Tunnel. Once on the mainland you can drive all the way to Milan on the motorway system; tolls can be expensive, particularly in Switzerland. At Italian frontier crossings you can buy booklets for fuel coupons and vouchers for motorway tolls. Italian motorways are called *autostradas* – all are toll roads. The *autostrada* system in northern Italy focuses on Milan, with motorways leading off to all the major lakes. Traffic congestion in Milan can be awful and motorists are advised to leave their cars in the ATM car parks on the outskirts. Sightseeing is easy using public transport: metro, buses, trams and trolleys. Motorists are advised to have comprehensive cover and an international green insurance card. In cases of breakdown, call ☎ **116**.

Milan can also be reached by **coach**. Eurolines run services from the UK and other European countries to Milan, Verona and Bergamo. For bookings and information in the UK, ☎ 020 7730 8235.

By train: the quickest rail route to Milan from the UK is by Eurostar to Paris, then the overnight service to Milan. Drivers can load their cars on the overnight **motorail** service at Bologna or Paris, arriving in Milan the following morning. Most trains arrive at Milan's **Stazione Centrale** (☎ freephone 1478 88088); from here buses and metro go to the city centre. The station has a tourist office, banks, restaurants, a supermarket and a 24-hour pharmacy.

What to Pack

Take strong shoes for walking around Milan and visiting the lake region. You'll need a sweater for the evenings (except Jul–Aug) and rainwear in spring and autumn. Do not wear shorts and beachwear when visiting churches. You can swim at the larger hotels and also many of the lake shores – so pack a costume. The Milanese are more formal in their dress than in other parts of Italy – it is the fashion capital of Europe and designer gear features strongly in leisure and casual wear.

Money Matters

ATMs are found everywhere and accept all major cards. **Credit or debit cards** can be used at hotels, restaurants, petrol stations and most shops. American Express **travellers' cheques** are widely accepted. **The euro** replaced the lira on 1 January 2002. It is issued in notes of 5, 10, 50, 100, 200 and 500 euros, and coins in denominations of 1, 2, 5, 10, 20 and 50 cents and 1 and 2 euros.

Accommodation

Hotels or *alberghi* are rated from 1–5 stars (depending on facilities, not service standards). *Pensioni* are more modest. Most hotels have different rates in summer and winter; some resort hotels in the lake region close in winter. Check if breakfast is included – you can usually get a cheaper, better meal in a bar. Lists of hotels and pensions are posted in tourist offices, but they are not obliged to make bookings. The decent hotels in Milan are often fully booked during trade fairs. Most hotels are in the city centre near Stazione Centrale and the Piazza della Repubblica. To book, contact Milano Hotels Central Booking, ✉ Piazza Missori, ☎ 02 805 4242. There are **youth hostels** (*Ostelli per la gioventu*) in Bergamo, Como, Mantua, Riva del Garda, Menaggio and Verona. Milan's

Piero Rotta hostel is at ✉ viale Salmoiraghi 2, ☎ 02 3926 7095. Italy's Youth Hostel Association is the *Associazione Italiana Alberghi per la Gioventu* (or AIG), ✉ Pallazzo della Civilta del Lavoro, Quadrato della Concordia, 00144 EUR Roma, ☎ 06 591 3702. An international membership card is needed, often obtainable at the hostel. Hostels are closed during the day and may have a curfew at night. They are renowned for noisy school parties, particularly around the Easter period.

Camping is popular. The lakes have fine waterside sites, but they are crowded and noisy in August. Milan has two sites on the outskirts of the city. Unofficial camping is frowned on by the police, but tourist offices have lists of official sites. To obtain a camping carnet and details of all Italy's camp sites, contact *Centro Internazionale Prenotazioni Campeggio*, ✉ Casella Postale 23, 50041, Calenzano, Firenze, ☎ 055 882 382.

Eating Out

Milan's restaurants serve food from China, India, Mexico and Japan, with the ubiquitous North American fast food, but do try some **Milanese specialities**. A *ristorante* offers antipasto, pasta, main course and dessert. Cheaper *trattorias* are much more likely to serve regional dishes. Specialist restaurants include *spaghetterias* and *pizzerias*. For snacks, try a *tavola calde* or *panini* bar.

Vegetarians are catered for at most eateries. Restaurants usually open from ⊕ 12:00–15:00 and from 19:30 onwards. Many restaurants close for one day a week, typically Sunday, though in the lake area it is more likely to be on Monday.

Transport

Getting around poses few problems, apart from traffic congestion in central Milan. **Road:** Milan has an efficient public transport system, which is fortunate as driving a car in the city is very difficult. Outside Milan, the *autostada* system allows you to reach all parts of the area more easily.

Car hire: Cars and camper vans (*autono-leggios*) can be hired at the main airports, where firms such as **Avis** (☎ 02 669 0280), **Hertz** (☎ 02 669 0061) and **Europcar** (☎ 02 8646 3454) have offices. It is cheaper to hire in advance from your own country. There is a minimum age limit of 21 and a credit card will be required.

Public transport: Milan's city transport system is operated by *Azienda Trasporti Municipali (ATM)*, with buses, trolley buses, trams and the metro. **Buses** and

trams are orange, and their stops are marked with yellow signs. They are frequent but often crowded. Buy tickets before boarding. The green *Tram Turistico* departs from Piazza Castello on a two-hour tour with multilingual taped commentary. Bus tours, run by Autostradale, depart from the cathedral square and last for three hours. Both tours are highly recommended. The **Metro** has four lines. Line one is shown on maps in red, line two in green, line three in yellow and line four (the latest) in blue. Trains run from ⏱ 06:00 to midnight. ATM tickets can be used for all types of transport, though they cannot be used twice on the metro. As well as day tickets, weekly and monthly passes can be bought; 24- or 48-hour tourist tickets are good value. Tickets must be bought in advance (from automatic machines,

tobacconists and newspaper kiosks).

Taxis: White in colour, taxis (expensive) cannot be hailed in the street and must be boarded at official taxi ranks scattered around the city. Make sure that the meter is switched on at the beginning of the ride. There will be surcharges for night-time journeys, luggage and trips to the airports.

Train: Italy's national railway, **FS** (*Ferrovie dello Stato*), is efficient and inexpensive. Routes link Milan with all the lakes. Tickets can be bought at the stations and at travel agents. A number of train passes are available. For exploring northern Italy by train the 'Travel at Will' (*Biglietto Turistico Libera Circolazione*) ticket is useful. Other passes include Flexicard and the Kilometrico. Details can be obtained from the Stazione Centrale and travel agents.

Boat: All the larger lakes are served by watercraft such as steamers, hydrofoils, paddle steamers and motor boats. Some are timetabled ferries for foot passengers or vehicles, while others cruise the lakes on excursions. Contact local tourist offices about daily or weekly passes. Services are curtailed in winter.

Cycles and motorbikes: Cycling is popular and bikes can be hired in all major towns. It is not recommended in Milan, despite the existence of cycle lanes, as motorists can be ruthless. Cycling around the lakes or in the Alpine foothills can make a delightful holiday. Motorbikes, mopeds and scooters can also be hired. Helmets are compulsory and there are minimum age limits. *The Globetrotter Travel Map of Milan and the Italian Lakes* is highly recommended. Free guides provided by tourist offices are good for general purposes. The Touring Club of Italy's *Lombardia* is good, as is their street plan of Milan.

Business Hours

Unlike in the south of Italy, the afternoon siesta is becoming more rare in the north. Most businesses in Milan work a 09:00–17:00 day. Shops close on Saturday afternoons and Sundays and some may take a lengthy lunch break. Most museums and galleries close on Mondays, but may stay open until 20:00 in summer. Chemists (*farmacias*) usually open ⏲ 09:30–19:30 Monday– Saturday. A rota for late and Sunday opening is posted in the windows of all chemists.

Tipping

A service charge and VAT are added to most restaurant and hotel bills; no tipping is needed unless service is outstanding. It is customary to tip porters, usherettes in cinemas, bellboys and attendants. A gratuity of 10 per cent is usual for taxi drivers and tour guides.

Time Difference

Italy uses Central European time, normally 1 hour ahead of GMT, 7 hours ahead of US Eastern Standard Time. From the last weekend of March to the end of September clocks are put one hour ahead.

Communications

Although the Italian **postal system** has a poor reputation, most post offices in Milan and the north of the country work efficiently. They open ⏲ 08:30–13:50 Mon–Fri and 08:30–12:00 Sat. There are post offices at Stazione Centrale and at Milan's two airports. Stamps can be bought at tobacconists. Public **telephones** are run by *Telecom Italia* and

there are plenty in Milan and around the lakes. Public phones take coins and cards (from tobacconists and newsstands). GSM mobile phones can be hired at the Euro Business Centre at Malpensa Airport. A Telecom Office at Stazione Centrale allows you to make international calls and also send and receive faxes. Milan's area code is 02. When dialling abroad from Italy, use 0044 for the UK, 001 for the USA, 00353 for Ireland, 0061 for Australia. **Internet Cafés** are appearing widely in Milan and other cities in the north of Italy.

Electricity

The supply is 220 volts and plugs have two or three round pins. Visitors should bring their own travel plug adapter from home.

Weights and Measures

Italy uses the metric system.

Health Precautions

Water is safe to drink and public fountains are plentiful. Bottled water is available too. **Food** in restaurants is normally hygienically prepared, but shellfish can cause upset stomachs. Prevent **sunstroke** by using a hat and a high-factor sunscreen. **Mosquitoes** can be a problem in the summer, so take an insect repellent.

Personal Safety

Though the lake region sees little crime, Milan, like many cities, does have petty theft. A few sensible precautions reduce the risk considerably. Carry only minimal cash and keep valuables in the hotel safe. Beware of pickpockets on crowded trains, buses and in public places. Avoid poorly lit places at night. Lock your car and never leave valuables on view. If you are a victim, report to the local police station (*questura*). Larger stations have a tourist department and can issue a report for your insurance company. The police emergency number is **113**.

Etiquette

Wearing beachwear or shorts in **churches** is offensive. Do not disturb worshippers during a service, particularly with flash photography. Milan is very fashion conscious; smart dress and formality are considered important. **Smoking** is banned on public transport (but usually tolerated in restaurants). Reaction to **topless sunbathing** varies, but it is usually not acceptable at hotel pools or on lakeside beaches.

Useful Words and Phrases
- Yes/No *Si/No*
- Please *Per favore*
- Thank you *Grazie*
- You're welcome *Prego*
- Good morning *Buongiorno*
- Good evening *Buona sera*
- Good night *Buena Notte*
- Excuse me *Mi scusi*
- Do you speak English? *Parla inglese?*
- I don't understand *Non capisco*
- Speak slowly *Parla lentamente*
- What/Who/Where? *Che?/Chi?/Dove?*
- How?/When?/Why? *Come?/Quando?/Perché?*
- Good *Buono*
- Bad *Male*
- Fast *Rapido*
- Slow *Lento*
- Big *Grande*
- Small *Piccolo*
- Hot *Caldo*
- Cold *Freddo*

Below: *Finding a postbox is easy in northern Italy.*

INDEX OF SIGHTS